THERE'S SOMEONE IN RECEPTION

Adventures in local journalism

By Alex Morrison

There's Someone In Reception: Adventures in local journalism

Copyright © 2024 Alex Morrison
Paperback Edition

All rights reserved. No part of this book may be used or reproduced by any means, graphic, electronic, or mechanical, including photocopying, recording, taping or by any information storage retrieval system without the prior written permission of the author except in the case of articles and reviews permitted by copyright law.

CONTENTS

Introduction: The Aubergenius	v
Chapter one. Walk-in wonders: Legless killer, lock switch dad & kidnapped tortoise	1
Chapter two. Show and tell: Stoneless roses, Edna's medal & grenade at Greggs	26
Chapter three. Animal, vegetable or mineral? Deadly jam, lucky duck & Nazi greyhound	47
Chapter four. Too good to be true? Bin Laden in Skegness	70
Chapter five. The walking dead: Mortality mix-ups	96
Chapter six. Reporters under fire: Hostage, handcuffs & 'fuck you too!'	112
Chapter seven. The ones that count	146
Chapter eight. Ring-ins & letters: Siege negotiator, stolen scarecrow & battle-tank surprise	164
Chapter nine. On patch: Brothel knocking, Croydon Christmas & pirates hate Britney	179
Chapter ten. Twin terrors: Death knocks & vox pops	208
Chapter eleven. Out of office: Doors shut, DMs open	227
Conclusion: Past, present and future	252
Appendix: Tweets	259
Author's Note	273

INTRODUCTION
The Aubergenius

IT STARTED WITH AUBERGINES.

In 2008, a man walked up a narrow flight of stairs and entered a cramped local newspaper office. Inside, he found four or five journalists. They were young – all in their twenties – so perhaps he expected them to look up eagerly. In fact, most of them stared resolutely at their computers, trying to look busy. Not discouraged, the visitor beamed around, clearly bursting to share good news. He had *a story* – a tale worth telling in the pages of the local press.

The journalists' lack of enthusiasm might seem strange, but it's understandable. The visitor had just become a "walk-in" – a person who turns up unannounced with a story they want printed, broadcast or otherwise shared with the world. As any reporter can attest, the percentage of walk-ins that result in great stories is not high. Front-page news can wander into reception (the first line of defence at most newspapers) but there is plenty of chaff for every grain of wheat. As a result, journalists can be sceptical – even cynical – when a walk-in walks in. If no reporter volunteers, the unwritten law of the journalistic jungle decrees that the newest trainee handles it. In this case, that reporter was me.

Less than a year into my first journalism job, at the *Crawley News* in West Sussex, I took my colleagues' hint and got up to meet the man. A few first impressions struck me simultaneously. He was remarkably animated, literally bouncing on the balls of his feet. He asked me to guess his age. I think I guessed about sixty-five, and he proudly announced he was seventy-eight. But the thing I noticed above all was the armful of aubergines.

I grabbed my notepad and persuaded him to sit down – an achievement on its own. Our open-plan office had no meeting room, so everyone pretended not to listen as I started the interview. The man, Antonio Massimo, explained that aubergines had helped him reach a conclusion that was still hotly debated in the wider world: our planet was getting warmer.

I can't remember my first reaction. I don't think he gave me time to form one. He spoke with an energy I can hardly remember seeing before or since, even among people decades younger. He was a living advert for eating home-grown food. He invited me to his allotment, from which he and his partner fed themselves and provided food for the local hospice. *Fair enough*, I thought. *Even if the climate change line doesn't work, "man grows food for hospice" is worth a page lead* (the main story on a newspaper page). Conscious that my colleagues were listening, I agreed to meet him at the allotment to continue the interview.

When I reached the plot – lush and beautifully ordered, like something from *Gardeners' World* – Mr Massimo explained his theory. He had come to Crawley from Italy (for reasons I can't remember) forty years earlier, and had repeatedly tried to grow aubergines, as he had in his homeland. For years, they simply would not grow. But over time, the plants did a little better, and now he had a bumper crop every year. To prove his point, he gave me some – so many, in fact, that I had to distribute them among my colleagues. I don't believe anyone thanked me.

Back at my desk, I wrote it up, complete with a grateful quote from the hospice (it's always reassuring to get verification of a story, especially if your source is somewhat eccentric). I sent it to the editor, who deserves a mention here. Glenn Ebrey came up with the headline for this gardener-scientist: "Aubergenius!"

And that was it. The story got published and I

moved on. That's how journalism works. But something about this one stayed with me. In many ways, Mr Massimo gave me a glimpse into the future – and not just by observing climate change. More than any other story I covered, this one started me thinking about something that – years later – inspired me to write this book. It's a classic example of why many people hold two (somewhat contradictory) views about local journalism: it's ridiculous and it really matters. In the UK at least, local papers and radio stations are simultaneously loved and laughed at. As well as general scorn for "the media", local journalism attracts a particular disdain. Mocking local news is a minor national sport, like badminton or glaring at queue-jumpers.

This strikes me as unfair for many reasons, the first of which is my unashamed love of local journalism. Secondly, mockery of local headlines usually implies the reporters involved don't see the funny side. As this book will show, they very much do. Of course, some headlines are unintentionally hilarious ("One-armed man applauds the kindness of strangers") but a reporter writing about a kidnapped tortoise (of which more later) covers the story *because* it's funny.

The funny side of Mr Massimo's story is obvious. But it matters too. It matters that a person can – or at least could – share something like this with their local community. It matters that the journalists who cover that community are – or at least were – accessible to the public. Most of all, it matters because people need to know, via reliable sources rather than social-media hearsay, what is going on in their villages, towns and cities. That might be an enthusiastic gardener sharing his wisdom and vegetables, a taxpayer angry with the council, or a desperate crime victim with nowhere else to turn.

Having pondered the mysterious case of Mr Massimo and his aubergines for over a decade, I tentatively pitched an idea on Twitter in January 2022:

Dear local newspaper journalists – past (like me) and present. We need a book of brilliant/bizarre "walk-in" stories. Working title: "There's someone in reception" (at which point everyone pretends to be working so someone else has to go). Who's got good material? #journorequest

I didn't expect much of a response, and for a couple of hours not much happened. Then it took off. Soon I had hundreds of replies, detailing an astonishing mix of stories spanning several generations. I had offered to write a book, and now it seemed a book must be written. Like all journalists pitching an ambitious story, part of me had hoped the editor would say no. *Oh well*, I thought, *I'd better get started.* I began picking through the replies, choosing the best and requesting interviews. Nearly everyone said yes. I was writing the book, but what sort of book should it be?

First and foremost, this is a book of walk-ins. It contains the experiences and insights of scores of journalists who kindly told me their tales. For me, the power of journalism comes from giving people a voice, letting them speak directly to the reader, listener or viewer. This was drummed into me from day one of journalism training, when my teacher wrote the following words – in gigantic letters – on a whiteboard: "No one gives a fuck what you think." Blunt, maybe, but I took it to heart: tell people's stories and leave your opinion out of it.

Full disclosure: as well as stories from my own career, this book contains observations and – worst of all – opinions. I had no choice. Organising so many disparate tales into a coherent narrative required a narrator, and sometimes a judge to sum up the opposing evidence. Like any decent journalist, I'll make a clear distinction between "news" and "comment", and I invite you to dismiss the latter with a disgusted tut. If that won't cover the depth of your feelings, I believe the classic move is to spit out your cornflakes.

Still, in honour of my rude but wise tutor, most of what follows comes from people who were there – journalists who (among many other things) rescued a duck from a van engine, got punched by a suspected hitman, and dressed up as an elf for an ill-advised Christmas feature. This book is a tribute to them and a celebration of their commitment to the people and places they serve. That's the double-edged sword of local news: you are far closer to your audience, far more exposed to them, than your national counterparts. This was especially true when most local journalists worked in offices on their patch, which meant the public could – and frequently did – walk through the door.

As demonstrated by my colleagues avoiding the infamous aubergine walk-in (and I admit I sometimes dodged walk-ins too), not all journalists love it when the public come to visit. You'll soon see why. However, a significant minority of the journalists interviewed for this book said they loved walk-ins and would gladly volunteer on hearing the immortal words: "There's someone in reception."

CHAPTER ONE

Walk-in wonders: Legless killer, lock-switch dad & kidnapped tortoise

"I DIDN'T HAVE MUCH on my news list, so I ran downstairs," said Benjamin Wright. It was 2006, and Wright – then a trainee at the *South Wales Evening Post* – was "enthusiastic about everything". That enthusiasm was about to pay off. In reception, he met a man and a woman, both in their twenties. The man began to speak, explaining that he had "accidentally" windsurfed from Swansea to Devon.

"I remember writing my shorthand notes and my pen just stopped," Wright said. "You think you are prepared for everything but it was like 'sorry, say that again'. The guy sort of downplayed it. He was a seasoned windsurfer and he had decided to go a little bit further than normal. I remember him saying 'I knew I had gone too far when I went past a tanker'. I put a star in the margin straight away [to make this key quote easy to find when writing the story up]." Finding himself far out to sea, the windsurfer had decided to go with the wind. Reaching the coast five hours later, he asked someone: "Where am I?" The locals welcomed him to Devon and took him to the pub, still in his wetsuit, where they bought him food and beer.

"Then he phoned his wife to ask if she could pick him up," Wright said. "Poor woman had a seven-hour round trip." Back in the newsroom, Wright's colleagues were amazed – but his editor wanted copy quickly for the next day's paper. "It was a bit of a panic. I had too much in my notebook – too many good lines that could each have made the intro." Despite the rush, Wright organised a photo of the windsurfer – posing with an A-Z map in classic local newspaper style – along with a disapproving quote from the Coastguard. Unsurprisingly, it made national news.

Wright said the experience taught him never to dismiss someone who walks into reception with a story. "I used to get told off for staying a long time in reception, but I let people have their time," he said. "My mum used to work in a nursing home and I would go to work with her sometimes as a kid. I would listen to people talking. That way of speaking – just chatting to someone to see what happens – is fine with me." He learned a similar lesson in his journalistic training – an "I'm OK, you're OK" approach in which the reporter "presents as being OK" to keep people calm, regardless of what they are saying.

"I always took people in good faith at the start," he added. "Even if they're talking total rubbish, it's good shorthand practice, and sometimes it's a funny story when you're back in the newsroom. One guy came in and sang his whole life to me – his life story in song."

Wright's willingness to chat – even off-duty – led him to find another surprising story at a petrol station. Meeting an old classmate from school, he noticed the man had his leg in plaster and asked him what had happened. During the explanation, the man mentioned that – despite the injury – he had played football at the weekend and "come off the bench and scored the winning goal against our local rivals". It was a header.

• • •

While Wright's windsurfer breezed in to see if the paper wanted to tell his tale, others demand their fifteen minutes of fame. Robert Barman was news editor of the *Kent Messenger* when the receptionist called from downstairs to say: "There's a guy here with a housing issue." So far, so normal. But the receptionist added: "Just so you know, he's superglued both his hands to the front counter."

Feeling he couldn't really send a reporter to handle this, Barman ventured downstairs. The visitor – a military veteran who said he was being evicted from his accommodation – was indeed glued to the counter. He wanted a story written, and evidently believed this was the best way to ensure success. Oddly, the paper had not refused – or even been asked – to run the story before this extreme action. As Barman told the man: "We would have spoken to you without you gluing your hands to the desk."

In fact, the adhesion of human skin to the front counter became more urgent than the housing issue, and Barman said the conversation moved on to how to release the man from his voluntary imprisonment. A long debate followed, involving paramedics and firefighters, during which time an audience gathered. Fearing what would happen when the man needed the toilet, Barman went upstairs and fetched washing-up liquid and the thinnest card in his wallet: his Blockbuster Video membership (note to younger readers: in the mists of prehistory – in this case 2003 – we used to visit a place called Blockbuster to physically borrow films to watch. We then had to return them or be fined. It was exhausting).

While some people might have been upset at being glued to their local newspaper office, Barman said their sticky visitor remained good humoured – and, even better, his bladder remained resolute. At last, with much encouragement from soap and now-extinct movie rental paraphernalia, he was freed. Barman doesn't recall the paper running a story on either the counter incident or the man's housing issue – but he said the housing provider was contacted and the troubled man got some leeway to stay in his accommodation, along with support from a veterans' charity.

Barman assumed this incident would be a one-off. In the years before and afterwards, nothing like it has happened – with one exception. Two weeks after the superglue incident, someone "came in and handcuffed himself to the rails on the front door", also due to a housing issue. Keen to avoid a repeat call to the emergency services, Barman asked: "Can you just unlock yourself?" The man produced the key and obliged. No need for the Blockbuster card.

In my days in local news, I often wondered why people walked in with deeply personal stories to share. Barman's examples provide part of the answer: they think the press has power. They're right. Local stories often lead to action by councils or other organisations, whose leaders may prefer to resolve an individual grievance to avoid negative publicity. Even if nothing can be done, telling a story publicly satisfies our deep sense of justice. I notice this in my children; if they feel they've been treated unfairly – perhaps receiving four chocolate buttons when a sibling got five – they need to be heard. The buttons may be gone, but the story *must* be told. That might sound flippant, but in the often-unfair adult world, journalists provide a real service by allowing people to speak. In local news, these stories sometimes seem trivial – potholes, parking, bin collections – but if someone cares enough to walk in, it clearly matters to them. It might matter to other people, too.

Some walk-ins simply want the publicity or attention of appearing in the paper. Like Mr Massimo and his aubergines, they have something to share with the entire town. Such visitors are often somewhat eccentric, and some bring stories so odd or unbelievable that they cannot – or should not – be printed (more on this later). Like several of the reporters I interviewed, I generally tried to find a printable story in every walk-in. It's not always easy.

• • •

"There's a man in reception who is doing a sponsored swim and wants to speak to you. He's got no legs and says he's a convicted murderer."

These words have made me laugh at least once a day since Polly Rippon first replied to my tweet. News stories usually open with the best or most interesting fact – and this call from reception spectacularly misses the news line. Surely "convicted murderer" is key here, followed by the killer's lack of legs. The sponsored swim – though undoubtedly remarkable in the circumstances – comes a distant third in a list of things I need to know about this person.

Rippon usually enjoyed the late shift at the *Sheffield Star*. "You were on your own a lot because most of the other reporters went home at four, but you did get a lot of good tales," she said. The arrival of a murderer brought this lack of backup into sharp focus, but curiosity trumped fear and she headed down the dingy stairwell to the grotty tradesman's entrance at the back of the building. She can't recall why reception sent the visitor round that way – but it might have been due to the security guard on duty there, who kept an eye on the reporters.

Armed with nought but a notepad, Rippon met the visitor while the security guard pretended not to watch. The swimming sensation explained that he had killed his former housemate, after the housemate had been convicted of a sexual offence against a child. Now out of prison – where he had lost his legs due to meningitis – he was planning a sponsored swim at Sheffield's Ponds Forge pool to raise money for a children's charity.

"I took his number and interviewed him there and then," Rippon said. "I knew I would have to check it out, so I went upstairs and looked him up in the paper's cuttings library." The backstory checked out: he had indeed killed his housemate, and the *Star* duly ran a piece on his sponsored swim. The sub-editor (the people who edit, write headlines and design pages) went with a no-nonsense headline: "Legless murderer swims for charity."

• • •

Swimming wasn't an option for a young man who, in the summer of 1981, found himself stranded outside his native UK without a passport. Jaine Blackman, then a reporter at Swindon's *Evening Advertiser*, got the story when the man's brother walked in and asked: "Would you get in trouble if your brother used your passport to get back to England?" She can't remember why he brought this enquiry to the local paper, but she soon saw a great story emerging. The man's brother had joined the French Foreign Legion and subsequently escaped – and he had in fact already crossed the

English Channel using his brother's passport.

"When he said his brother was already back in England, I rushed out to interview him and called the story back from a phone box to meet a noon deadline," Blackman said. After fleeing the Foreign Legion, the brother had gone to Corsica, where he had "shacked up with a maid, and was sharing a room with her friends – four other maids," Blackman said. "He had then left to come back to Swindon, hitch-hiking and hiding in train toilets, and made his way to Calais. His brother in England had then sent his passport over, as they looked similar." The ruse had worked – and Blackman's story made the front page.

The *Advertiser*'s reporters ran a pool system to sell their stories to the nationals, and this one sold to the *News of the World*. "They sent a reporter down and I was given a day to go and hang out with him and the two brothers," Blackman said. "I sat in on the interview. A day later, the *News of the World* reporter called me up. He said he'd forgotten to ask whether the man had 'shagged any of the maids'. I had to go back and ask that question. He said he had."

In the days of print-first local newspapers, reporters often tried to sell stories to the national press. I was never entirely clear on the rules around this, but it was quietly allowed as long as your own paper published the story before you gave it to anyone else. With modest pay as a local reporter (I started on £13,000 a year) selling stories was tempting, both for the money and for building contacts with national papers, where many reporters wanted to work. In theory, you could sell to any national paper – but in my experience the stories that sold tended to be tabloid tales like Blackman's maids.

Blackman joined the *Advertiser* in 1979, and quickly became "queen of the front office walk-ins". She said: "I was the junior reporter – the only trainee they had taken on in a long time – so I basically got sent down every time. Everyone else hated it, but I never minded going down to reception. Nine times out of ten there would be no story and you would be subjected to a mad rant or could refer someone to the right person to address their issue. But the tenth time… well, that was golden."

One such nugget came when a man walked in and said: "I want you to write a story saying I'm not a paedophile." Explaining his reasons for wanting this worrying clarification, he told Blackman that he had both a wife and a teenage girlfriend. The former was dying of cancer; the latter was pregnant with his baby. Surprisingly, the two women had become close friends – and the younger woman was acting as carer during the older woman's illness. Blackman kept in touch with the trio, and it led to a story that began with the words: "A wife, dying of cancer, spent her last moments clinging to the hand of her husband's pregnant teenage mistress."

Blackman is glad to have learned her trade in the 1970s and 80s – and not just because of the subsequent loss of town-centre receptions and walk-ins. "My God, it was good training," she said. "Sometimes a senior reporter would rip the paper out of my typewriter and read it out. It was tough, but you learned fast. You didn't make the same mistake twice."

• • •

In the mid-2010s, Ewan Foskett manned a desk at a community hall for the *Welwyn Hatfield Times* to "get some stories and show that we were about in town". Many papers use similar methods to maintain a local presence despite office closures, but Foskett said it rarely led to good stories. The time was often spent twiddling thumbs or writing up existing work.

This scepticism can only have increased after the visit of a local councillor. The man had no story. He just popped in to say hello. Foskett recalled that the conversation turned to rugby, at which point the councillor "burst into 'Bread of Heaven' out of nowhere". He described the man's voice as "middling to fair", adding: "What he lacked in technical ability, he made up for in passion."

After finishing the song, the councillor "farted very loudly". An awkward pause followed. Would the man acknowledge what had just happened? No. "He just looked at me and left," Foskett said. They never saw each other again. Commenting on the eccentricity of people who visit the local paper, Foskett said the timing – usually during office hours – might be a factor. As he put it: "All the normal people are at work."

• • •

If wasting a journalist's time was a criminal offence, that singing councillor would share a cell with a tattoo artist who visited Devin Wilger at *Yorkton This Week* in Saskatchewan, Canada, in the late 2010s. The visitor – a huge man with tattoos covering most of his body – wanted to talk about a very important issue: chairs.

"I take him into a side room to talk, not sure what his story actually is," Wilger said. "He starts telling me the story of how he went to a local dentist, and when he got to the dentist's chair he saw that the fabric on the armrest was worn and starting to crack. This made him very angry, because he thought dentists shouldn't be allowed to have a worn-out armrest on their chair."

I know what you're thinking: Hold the front page! But wait. There's more. The tattoo artist explained he could "never have a bad armrest" on his chair – and if a health inspector saw such a thing, he would be "shut down immediately". Wilger said the man "talked about his dentist having a kind of shit chair for something like forty minutes".

"With nothing verifiable and it mostly being a guy going off about having to have a nicer chair than the dentist, I couldn't really do anything with it," Wilger said. "I'm also pretty sure he kept the dental appointment anyway in spite of the bad armrest."

. . .

Adrian Moss paints a vivid picture of life in a district outpost of the *South Yorkshire Times* in the 1970s.

"It was a tiny office. It would fail health and safety nowadays," he said. "Four of us in a broom cupboard of a room. Sit-up-and-beg typewriters, outside toilet, and the two older journalists smoking massive King Edward cigars while they typed." Walk-ins were common, he said. "But it wasn't always people with a story about the biggest cabbage on the allotment, or a photo of a turnip that looked like Max Bygraves who came through the door. A whole gang of contributors would visit that tiny office in the mining town of South Elmsall. Women's Institute news, obituary notices, completed wedding forms, and even the weekly news from the Royal Antediluvian Order of Buffaloes."

Reflecting on this period of his career, Moss said: "Those halcyon days will never be repeated. Young people today would never believe what it was like to be a part of the community as a local newspaper reporter was back then." Some of the reporters interviewed for this book – especially those still working today – say they remain deeply embedded in the communities they cover. But the landscape of local news has undeniably changed. Over the last two decades, print sales and advertising income have plummeted amid the unstoppable rise of online news and social media. Most local papers tried to embrace the digital revolution, and a few have succeeded, but local journalism has been transformed since the time Moss described. Most newspaper offices have closed, so most reporters now either work remotely or from large hub offices – often far from the area they cover. While the effects of this on journalists and journalism can be debated, the impact on walk-ins is clear: there's hardly anywhere to walk in.

That deprives us of walk-ins such as the bus driver who visited Moss at the *Doncaster Evening Post* in the late 1970s. The driver wanted the paper to write something about his "serious problem": people kept calling him Adolf Hitler for no apparent reason. "Of course, the collective newsroom ears pricked up," Moss said. "And, when he came up into the newsroom, yup, he was small, had slicked black hair and a tiny moustache." In short, he was the spitting image of Hitler. The headline? "Please don't call me Adolf."

. . .

Like Moss, Tim Robinson describes a world of local news that is barely recognisable today. In 1991, Robinson was a trainee reporter at the *Bucks Herald* in Aylesbury. The office was in the town centre, with ten reporters and the printing press on site. "You could write your story upstairs in the office, and every week you would hear the presses rolling," Robinson said. He saw the paper being printed, copies going out and people buying them. Walk-ins were common, with a stream of visitors every day, providing a "brilliant connection with readers that you just don't have any more", he said. "I have brilliant memories about this. It's the stuff of being a reporter for me."

It wasn't all good, of course. There was a death threat (related to a court story the paper had published), followed swiftly by a block of concrete through the window – although this was caught on CCTV, landing the perpetrator in prison for a month. Still, walk-ins were mostly welcome and reporters "would enthusiastically go down because you never knew what you would hear".

One day, Robinson's enthusiasm was tested by the following call from downstairs: "There's a man in reception who burnt down County Hall and has just been released from Broadmoor [high-security psychiatric hospital]." Robinson sensed a "sort of ripple going around" among his more experienced colleagues. There had been a fire at County Hall more than two decades earlier. Robinson admitted being nervous on the way downstairs, but he was also intrigued.

The man in reception was indeed the 1970 County Hall arsonist. He had come to tell his story and to apologise to the people of the town. He described a difficult childhood, culminating in the arson at the age of eighteen. He did it because County Hall housed a court, where he had appeared as a defendant charged with a minor offence. More than twenty years on, the

Herald had a moving tale of remorse and rehabilitation. "We did a whole thing on him and his recovery and how he had come back to the town," Robinson said. "He was genuinely sorry."

. . .

Journalists want to help walk-ins, but they need something in exchange: a story. After a decade in journalism, and almost as long as a university press officer, I'm still surprised at how many people have absolutely no "news sense" (the ability to spot a good story, and to pick which part should be the headline). Plenty of non-journalists have an instinctive eye for stories, but some people literally wouldn't know a story if it happened in front of them. If a walk-in belongs to the latter group, the journalist's role is to sift through the haystack ("I grow lots of vegetables") to find a needle ("I discovered climate change using aubergines").

In 1994, *Northampton Chronicle and Echo* reporter Ben Hatch went to reception to meet a walk-in. Hatch cannot remember exactly what story the man wanted to tell, but a few minutes into the conversation, the visitor delivered a gift-wrapped headline. The man, a World War Two veteran, said a piece of shrapnel had been lodged in his bum since the Battle of Arnhem – and it had begun "moving around" fifty years to the day after this injury. "It was the splash [lead story on the front page] the next day," Hatch said.

Moving to the *Leicester Mercury* the following year, Hatch said "silly" stories somehow seemed to fall to him – although his new editors were often unimpressed. They saw the *Mercury* as the "paper of record", he said, and they hated the quirky tales he unearthed. These included a letter from a reader who claimed to have dug up "six perfectly preserved mince pies" while replanting a tree in a garden. Hatch was instructed not to write it up.

He got the same order for a twisting tale about a tortoise and a priest's son, who I'll call Jo. Jo had embarked on gender reassignment surgery. Jo's girlfriend, who was not informed about this in advance, responded by ending the relationship. In a bizarre bid to win her back, Jo kidnapped her tortoise and sent a ransom note – complete with some straw from the tortoise's bedding. With the news desk (a collective term for the editors) unmoved, Hatch reluctantly let the story go – instead pitching it to a local freelancer, who wrote it for the *Daily Star*, where it made the front page. Freelancers inevitably have better contacts than local reporters, so selling a story this way spares you the pain of cold-calling a national news desk – which to me was intimidating and often fruitless. On the downside, the freelancer will take a sizeable chunk of any fee.

Hatch admitted dealing with walk-ins could be a nightmare, but some of his best stories came that way. "Sometimes it's a relief going down to reception because you never know if it will be an absolute gem," he said. Giving an example from his first journalism job at the *Bucks Herald*, Hatch said he wrote a splash about a man who walked into a Mercedes showroom to ask for a small car part, possibly a wiper blade, because God was about to give him this particular car but this part would be faulty. Asked about how the story ended, Hatch said: "I don't think he ever got the car. We kept an eye on it for a while but the car never emerged."

※ ※ ※

One day in the 2000s, Ellen Beardmore – then a trainee, and therefore doomed to deal with walk-ins – answered the door at the *Pontefract and Castleford Express*. The visitor was a very ordinary man in his forties.

"He was a bit nervous, but people often were – it's a big deal going to the local paper," Beardmore said. "I sat him down and he said, 'I've had my wallet stolen'. He was quite reluctant to tell me all the details." The man explained he had been "with a woman" and later realised his wallet had vanished. "I had no clue what he was getting at," Beardmore said. Eventually, he explained that the woman in question was a "lady of the night", who took his wallet after he paid for her services.

Surprised the man wanted his story in the paper, Beardmore explained he would have to be named and pictured. "He didn't want that," she said. "We parted ways, and I don't think he ever got his wallet back."

• • •

Not every walk-in suffers from such shyness. One remarkably unabashed man visited the *Newcastle Evening Chronicle* in the late 1990s, with an issue that might have made an ordinary person pass out due to excessive blushing. The paper's office opened directly onto the city's famous Bigg Market, and the reception staff handled most visitors – only calling a reporter downstairs for good stories or especially tricky customers.

In this case, reception called and Dave Clark, then a trainee, went to see if the walk-in had a tale to tell. He did indeed. Clark said the man was "fairly aggressive" and "wild-eyed", sporting a grey beard and an anorak. Speaking in a strong Newcastle accent, the man said some gas engineers had stolen his collection of pornographic magazines while working at his home. These were no ordinary magazines. They were, the man explained, "Illegal stuff, really hardcore. Imported from Germany." Many walk-ins arrive with a bag of documents, but Clark said this man brought no "supporting materials".

Some people might have hesitated to tell this tale to a stranger, let alone ask them to publish it in a newspaper. But this visitor was not at all sheepish. He wanted his magazines back, and believed publicity was the best route. "I tried to talk him down," Clark said. "I tried to give him a clue about what this would be like." He told the man that his name, age and profession would have to feature in print, hoping this would make him think again. But the man remained set on his moment in the limelight. Clark said: "In the end I had to kick him out. I said, 'look, sir, I'm not going to do the story. You're going to have to go away'."

. . .

Facing such demands, journalists might feel tempted to

change the locks and unplug the phone. But they'd miss out on stories like a bizarre lock-switching saga covered by Mandy Langley at the *South Wales Argus* in 1988. It began when a woman arrived to complain about the council not rehousing her friend, who had just had a baby.

"Sounded routine," Langley said, but she arranged to visit the new mother. Finding the woman sitting dejected on the sofa with her baby, she took some notes. Then an incredible detail emerged: "She told me her husband had changed the locks on their flat while she was in hospital having their child."

This kind of line – a bombshell that turns a standard story into a stunning one – can almost stop a journalist's pen in mid-shorthand. Langley kept going. She got the full scoop, which was published under the headline: "Lock switch shocker for young mum." Somehow, she also persuaded the villain of the piece to be interviewed. "I remember going to see the husband, in what had been their flat, in some trepidation as to how I'd be received," Langley said. "He was actually OK; gave me his side of the story quite calmly."

Asked what his story was, Langley explained: "The marriage wasn't in good shape… he said that when the locks were changed, he didn't know she had gone into hospital. He'd only learned that from someone else, after the baby was born. He wanted to see the baby, but he also wanted a divorce."

• • •

Many reporters struggle to display that sort of calm when unwanted visitors approach. Frank Horsley remembers many "well-meaning menaces [who] managed to breach the receptionist's defences". Reflecting on thirty-nine years working in every editorial role from reporter to production editor at the *Worthing Herald* series (a group of related local newspapers), he said: "Goodness knows what proportion of your career you spent having your ear bent, with not a single column millimetre to show for it."

Working in Shoreham, he said his team had a "mixed relationship" with the leader of a local youth group, who would "regularly breeze into the office and regale us with details of her little darlings' latest show". The woman in question was kindly, but Horsley said there was "only so much enforced jollification a reporter – and a hungover one, to boot – can take".

He said the paper had a brilliant Lancastrian receptionist called Bet, who "could easily have been a character from *Coronation Street*". He added: "She would wave cheerily to well-known awkward customers as they walked past our front shop window and then exclaim 'piss off!' in celebration at their not entering the office." One day, Bet warned Horsley that the youth group leader was approaching, and he "leaped out of the office window and legged it up the back path".

Horsley once asked a colleague – with envy and admiration – how he had got rid of a notorious time waster who had arrived in reception. The colleague replied: "He fell for the oldest one in the book. I told him to write a letter to the editor."

Despite the drawbacks, Horsley said the long hours of dealing with walk-ins – often playing "agony aunt or uncle to people who had too much time on their hands" – were worth it for the "journalistic pearls that regularly fell into your copy tray". An example arrived one morning, not long after the pubs opened.

"A regular interrupted his first of the day at the Ferry Inn to stroll up the street, walk into our office and casually announce: 'Have you heard? The pub parrot's eaten all the charity cash'," Horsley said: "The disgraced Norwegian blue, or whatever it was, had dipped its beak into a pint mug on the bar containing a bundle of banknotes donated by regulars towards the local lifeboat and reduced them to papier-mâché.

Suffice it to say the story was that week's front-page lead, complete with a photograph reconstructing the crime."

CHAPTER TWO

Show and tell: Stoneless roses, Edna's medal & grenade at Greggs

AMONG THE MANY JOURNALISTIC TIPS and tricks I heard while interviewing people for this book, one stands above the rest. It relates to the surprisingly common phenomenon of people walking in with a bag – usually a carrier bag – full of documents. The rule is this: "The more crowded the plastic bag, and the more yellow the paper, the worse the story will be." Although I had never heard this before, nor directly thought these words, it instantly struck me as true. I thought back to meetings with conspiracy theorists, serial complainers and people obsessed with their neighbours' hedges encroaching over boundaries. I realised the weight and discolouration of documents was indeed strongly correlated with story crapness.

One of our regular visitors at the *Crawley News* seemed to have discovered a lost city of yellowing parchment, on which he scrawled an astonishing volume of hand-written notes. These were slammed down on our desks with the dramatic confidence of a TV lawyer producing case-winning evidence. I don't remember every claim he made. They were rich and varied. I still have one letter, which accuses Crawley's councillors of being werewolves (something the council never specifically denied).

While an untidy stack of documents borne into reception would send some reporters scuttling for the back stairs, many classic walk-ins involve a prop or artefact. Indeed, possession of a vital item might be the reason someone walks in rather than phoning. Conor Gogarty recalls such a story from his first journalism job at the *Essex Chronicle* and *Brentwood Gazette*. The newspapers were based in an edge-of-town business park that Gogarty likened to the set of the Ricky Gervais series *The Office*. Walk-ins were rare, but one day in 2017 a man buzzed the door and Gogarty went down to the entrance area the papers shared with another company.

"I have an image of him standing there in the lobby with a Tesco Bag for Life," he said. The man seemed fairly relaxed about the contents of the bag – which became surprising, when he removed a concrete plaque bearing text in German, the year 1947, the letters "SS" and a Swastika.

"As soon as he showed me the plaque, I thought 'this is way better than I have been led to expect from most walk-ins'," Gogarty said. The man explained that he had found the plaque as a child in 1970 while playing with friends beside a stream in Chelmsford. It bore the words: "Es lebe unser führer" (long live our leader) and the man told Gogarty he believed it had been carved by a German prisoner of war. The man agreed to pose for a picture and a video beside the stream, and the story earned Gogarty a byline in the *Daily Mirror*.

Job done. But bizarre stories often have many facets, and one detail still plays on Gogarty's mind. In a throwaway comment that Gogarty now wishes he had investigated further, the man mentioned that he was about to move house for "a bit of a change" – either to Glasgow or Walton-on-the-Naze. Exactly why the shortlist of destinations contained this unlikely pair, we may never know.

Gogarty only recalls one other walk-in during his year-long stint in Essex. It involved a verbose doctor with a stack of paperwork who wanted to discuss his case against a local hospital for unfair dismissal. Perhaps overenthusiastic after the Nazi plaque walk-in, Gogarty spent four hours with the man before his editor "turned up and made an excuse of why I needed to leave at that moment". The dispute did make a short story when the case concluded – some time after Gogarty had moved on to the *Bristol Post* – but he said meeting this paperwork-wielding visitor gave him a more balanced view of what walk-ins would be like. He added: "It's very rarely simple with walk-ins."

While Gogarty loved walk-ins – the "unpredictability of people just knocking on your door" and the ripple of laughter as everyone waits for someone else to get up and see who's knocking – he does not believe their demise is fatal for local news.

"Our inbox is full of people getting in touch with us with stories," he said. "They're just doing it in a different way." He said age-old techniques like going out "on patch" (see chapter nine), combined with newer sources like social media, provide a rich mix of stories "as long as you make the effort to speak to the person or meet up with them".

• • •

A complex backstory – also linked to a troubling artefact from World War Two – led a man to visit the *Widnes Weekly News* in the late 1970s. Dave Candler, then a teenaged trainee reporter, got a call from downstairs and went to meet the man.

"The guy was middle-aged and he was holding a shoebox," Candler said. "He was very sombre and serious, and he said the story he wanted to talk about had been on his mind for many years, since he was a child. It was clearly to do with the box, so I asked him what was inside. He said it was part of the skull of a World War Two German pilot. I just looked at him. I didn't particularly want to see inside the box, but I was a new reporter and I was learning that you have to find out everything you can. There was a piece of cloth inside. Between the folds there was a piece of bone. I was a little unnerved. I didn't know what to do. I wanted advice from my editor, so I went back upstairs and explained what was going on in reception. The editor came down and took the guy's details, and the man told us more about how he got the piece of skull. During the war, when he was a child, he had gone with friends to where a German bomber had crashed in Widnes playing fields. The plane had burned and it took a day or two for the flames to die down. After that he went in – as kids probably did back then – and found a pilot's flying helmet. Part of the pilot's skull was still inside. I think he was afraid to tell anybody about it. He thought he might get in trouble."

Candler said the man clearly felt guilty for keeping the skull for more than thirty years, tucked in a shoebox in a chest of drawers. He added: "I think we helped to relieve him of that guilt." The man agreed to tell the police about the skull fragment, which was later handed to the UK Ministry of Defence, who passed it to their German counterparts. A military burial was conducted, although the pilot's identity remained unknown.

Candler said the story shows the value of journalism because the man had found no way to air his secret for three decades, and finally turned to the local paper. It also demonstrates why so many strange stories end up in local news: with no obvious resolution available, people ask a journalist to make sense of a problem. Organising information is a fundamental part of the job, and in doing so a journalist may help people organise it in their own minds. Evelyn Waugh wrote: "To understand all is to forgive all." In light of Candler's story on the skull fragment, its keeper's actions are entirely forgivable.

• • •

At the risk of this book becoming an accidental history of Twentieth Century wars, the next tale goes further back in time, to World War One, via a local newspaper walk-in in 1998. It was Richard Edwards' first week as a trainee reporter on the *Pocklington Post* in East Yorkshire. A quiet, elderly lady called Edna Blackburn turned up – and gave him the first memorable story of his career.

"She just came in holding this object, but she didn't really say anything to anyone," he said. "I just started chatting to her." Edwards' colleagues were listening, and an incredible story unfolded. It turned out that Mrs Blackburn's husband had – during his childhood – lost a World War One medal belonging to his father.

"Eighty years after it was lost, a metal detectorist found it and dug it up – and from the name on the side, he traced it to a nearby war memorial," Edwards said. "The detectorist then rang up the only person in the local phonebook with the name Blackburn." This turned out to be Mrs Blackburn's grandson, who knew the story of the lost medal and directed the detectorist to his grandmother.

Mrs Blackburn, her grandson and the detectorist all gave interviews, and the story ran in the *Pocklington Post* and went national in *The Times*. The touching tale of the medal's return inspired Edwards and gave him confidence that he could hack it in his new career.

Like so many others, the Pocklington office Mrs Blackburn walked into is long gone. "With that has gone the opportunity for people to walk in and tell these wonderful, wonderful stories," Edwards said. However, he – like so many of the people interviewed for this book – remains a staunch supporter of local newspapers. He buys the *Selby Times* every week. "Long may they [local newspapers] be with us," he said.

• • •

Reporters have no control over the items people choose to bring in. In fact, some visitors aren't even sure what they are carrying, as Paul McElroy discovered.

"Somewhere around the late sixties, I was a young reporter on the *Bucks Advertiser* in Aylesbury when our receptionist Sally came into the newsroom from the front desk of our offices in Bourbon Street to tell us there was a 'gentleman at the desk with stuff in a box he thought might interest us'," McElroy said. "I went through to speak to him, a rustic old fellow with a heavy Bucks accent who told me he'd been clearing out his farmhouse."

The man had found a box of glass photograph transparencies that had belonged to his father. He didn't have room or use for them, so he suggested the paper should bin them if they were not of interest.

McElroy continued: "I took the box with about a hundred brown glass slides, each about six inches square, into the newsroom and asked a photographer if we could have a look at them on his darkroom enlarger. The first slide seemed a bit disappointing. It [was] just a bloke shearing a sheep. There were four or five of us crammed into the darkroom, looking over the photographer's shoulder."

Then the sports editor coughed and said: "Er, not entirely certain he's actually shearing that sheep." The chief reporter – who was "not a woman who shocked easily" – added: "Christ! He's...!" The man in the photograph was, to put it as politely as I can, engaged in a sexual act with the farm animal. McElroy continued: "The rest of the box was equally graphic, if slightly less unnatural, but we'd just been gifted a hoard of Victorian porn that would have made Hugh Hefner blush. Needless to say, they never made the paper and were supposedly thrown out, but I suspect they may still be stashed away somewhere in a newsroom locker."

. . .

One item that is definitely not stashed in a newsroom locker arrived at the *Pontefract and Castleford Express* in 2011. Reporter Hannah Postles was at work in the Pontefract office when a colleague from the advertising department, based in the Castleford office, called to say: "A man just walked in and whacked a hand grenade down on the counter." The visitor had found the grenade while walking in the woods, and wanted the paper to do a story. Advertising had hastily directed him to the police station, and the man had left a phone number before picking up his grenade and leaving. But then he came back, saying Castleford Police Station was closed and he would take it to Pontefract instead.

"Our office was near the police station, and we were quite concerned that he might call in to us first," Postles said. "We put down the shutters, so it looked like we were closed. We called the police and said, 'there might be a man with a grenade in his pocket on his way to you'." As it turned out, the police managed to contact the man before he set off for Pontefract.

"He had stopped at Greggs for a steak bake then popped home to eat it. While he was there, he got a call from the police," said Postles. "They told him to put the grenade on the table and leave. He took his cat and left, and his neighbours were also evacuated. The bomb squad went in and discovered it was a realistic replica."

When Postles interviewed the man afterwards, he

said he had initially thought the grenade was a toy – and in any case its pin was intact, so he thought it would be OK. He had left it in his van overnight, before deciding to take it to the local paper. Postles recalls careful deliberation about how the story was written up. "We didn't mention our involvement," she said. "We didn't want more people to bring in grenades."

• • •

Sometimes a walk-in cannot carry the thing they want to show you, so they ask you to come out and see it. This was the case for Wynford Emanuel, a trainee reporter at the *Rhondda Leader* in 1973. He was called to reception to meet a man who said he was fed up with his car, which had "fault after fault after fault". In fact, the Ford Escort had caused him so much trouble that he had decided to burn it.

Leaving the Tonypandy office – which smelled of solvents due to sharing the premises with a washing machine repair company – Emanuel and a photographer went with the man to see what he would do. "Whether I should have gone is another matter, but I did," Emanuel said. The man led them to some waste ground and got to work. "He poured petrol all over the car and set fire to it, and we stood there and watched it burn." The car was soon a charred hulk. Looking back almost fifty years on, Emanuel said this experience was an "interesting way to start working life".

In another strange moment early in his career, Emanuel was sent to a house fire near the office and arrived to find it still ablaze. "A man was coming out of the bedroom window," he said. "The only thing the man was wearing was a very short vest. Watching this… two elderly ladies were standing next to me. One said, 'I think it's disgusting leaving the house like that'."

· · ·

On the subject of curious episodes from 1970s Britain, Phil Mellows – then a trainee at the *Stratford Express* – met an "eccentric-looking chap" who walked in and introduced himself as the "unofficial historian of the Woolwich Ferry".

"I remember thinking I'd be more impressed if he was the official historian, but that wasn't why he was here," Mellows said. The man told him: "I'd like you to come and see my rose garden." Mellows asked if the garden had won prizes, to which the man replied: "No, I've removed all the stones. It's taken me ten years, I've worn out several sieves, but I've done it." When asked why, the man replied: "Stands to reason, it helps the drainage."

Not convinced by this logic, Mellows nonetheless went to the man's house in East Ham, along with photographer John Curtis. "There wasn't much for him to photograph, just a very tidy rose garden. It's hard to capture the absence of something," Mellows said. But then the eager gardener disappeared into his shed and came out with "the last bucket of stones". Sometimes a picture makes a story, and this one made a centre spread.

Later, in his second job at the *Ilford Recorder*, a less amusing walk-in led Mellows to leave local journalism. It started in standard fashion, with a call to meet a man downstairs in reception. "He was somewhat dishevelled and unshaven, but he had a kind of proud, almost aristocratic bearing," Mellows recalled. "We had featured him in a number of court reports after he'd been repeatedly arrested for being drunk… He told me he was trying to dry out, but the shame of our latest story had driven him back to the bottle. I was shocked. I apologised but could do nothing but mutter some platitudes about reporting the news. Shortly afterwards I handed in my resignation. The truth was I was already unhappy, and this was the final straw. I could play the tough and cynical hack, but I didn't want to do that. I went into full-time education, did a couple of degrees, and on returning to London got a job on the *Morning Advertiser*, writing about, ironically, pubs and drinking. I'm still doing it."

. . .

Sam Blackledge must have felt like quitting. He had been too slow to duck when the receptionist came looking for a reporter, and now he had been forced to spend ten minutes – "ages", as he experienced it – staring at a photograph. The picture's owner watched Blackledge eagerly, urging him to say what he could see. What could he see? Nothing. Just a bruise on a man's arm. Blackledge kept saying "no". He simply couldn't see whatever the man expected him to.

"Eventually," Blackledge said, "he revealed that he thought it looked like Jesus." The man said fifty percent of people could see the son of God, while the other half "can't or won't". Blackledge was in the latter camp and – having studied the picture from all angles – I am too. Jesus remains conspicuous only by his absence, for me at least.

Still, the man had made the effort to bring the picture (the bruise had since healed) to the *Plymouth*

Herald, and Blackledge thought readers would enjoy sorting themselves into Jesus and no-Jesus spotters. And, like so many weird walk-ins, this one contained joyous extra details. The man revealed that the bruise emerged after a friend bit him during a "play fight". He also told Blackledge the experience contributed to his decision to join a church, and he now relished the "opportunity to further Christ's message" (presumably not by biting people).

Blackledge said tales like the Jesus bruise are "less about the actual story and more about the fact he was such a character". He added: "That's what I love about local journalism. We are so privileged to meet these people and speak to them and share their stories."

• • •

At the *West Lancashire Evening Gazette* in the early 1980s, the privilege of dealing with walk-ins usually fell to trainee reporter Paul Burnell. This included meeting a man with a "weird US-Lancashire accent", who arrived with a record in his hand. Burnell sampled the musical contents, which he described as a "vanity record of cowboy songs". He added: "You've never heard anything so dire in your life." Like many reporters in such a situation, Burnell decided the easiest path was to write something, so he included a mention of the record in the paper's diary column, complete with a picture of the Wild West musician holding his record at the seafront.

Burnell also recalled one lady who walked in to tell him people were stealing her furniture and replacing it with "identical furniture – but it's not the same". Struggling to send the woman on her way, he was rescued by his editor: "Paul, you're needed upstairs."

. . .

In a sense, the role of a local journalist is simple: find and report on stories that matter to your readers. But, as this book shows, dealing with the public is rarely simple. A baffling variety of people arrive with an even more baffling variety of stories, opinions, problems and complaints. A single-minded journalist could just ask themself: is this a story? If not, tell the visitor to go away. In reality, the story/non-story lines are often blurred – and sympathy, decency, awkwardness and a host of other motives might prompt a reporter to do more than simply report. Very often, someone just needs to speak. Many times in my career, a walk-in would rant or cry about a problem – but, having done so, they didn't really want a story in the paper. Other times, journalists find themselves drawn into stranger roles. This book is littered with examples, from calling local councils about people's housing issues to negotiating with an armed man during a siege.

But the gold medal might go to Kahn Johnson, who gave up the entire summer of 1997 because of a walk-in. Johnson had joined the *Stamford Mercury* on work experience and managed to secure a full-time job, which allowed him to leave his previous employment at a bucket factory. In spring 1997, about six months into his journalistic career, he was still brimming with enthusiasm when a man from the Stamford Shakespeare Company – a well-known amateur group – walked into the office.

An actor had pulled out of their forthcoming production, and Johnson said the company wanted to publish a desperate appeal for local actors, as they were weeks away from showtime. To skip ahead a couple of acts, Johnson spent that summer performing in *The Merry Wives of Windsor*. Most reporters would have listened sympathetically and written a story. Not Johnson. Despite limited acting experience – a primary school play and one year of GCSE drama – he asked whether he could audition and was told he could. Surprised to be offered the role, he gladly accepted. "I just thought it might be something fun to do," he said.

He spent many evenings and Sundays rehearsing the role of Fenton, who he called the "least interesting character in the play". Then the show opened, with Johnson required to wear a "felt jacket and trousers and a weird hat". Johnson recalled a "terrifying night" when the *Mercury* news team came to watch. He was still the new guy in the office, and he suspected his colleagues were baffled by his decision to act in the play. He was also in a new relationship at the time, meaning he had to tell his partner: "Oh, by the way, I'm about to go and start doing this really stupid thing." Still, he enjoyed it, and joined a different company for a play the following year – but it didn't live up to his summer of Shakespeare.

* * *

For Isaac Ashe, the "golden age" of walk-ins came during his six years at the *Loughborough Echo*, from 2007-13. His long-serving editor "cared deeply about the paper", and as a weekly publication there was time for walk-ins, as well as long meetings to discuss plans and priorities. In one such meeting, it was decided that "sex sells". As Ashe recalled it, the message was: "Let's try to get a little bit more sex in the paper". The reporters took up the challenge enthusiastically, peppering the pages with nibs (news in brief) about "slightly dodgy" adverts from Craigslist.

But the climax of the sex drive came when a reader called the office to say he had created a "BDSM bed" (Google gives a range of results on the meaning of BDSM, including bondage, discipline, dominance, submission, sadism and masochism... but you get the idea). Reporter Matt Jarram arranged an interview, but the bed's inventor went one better – he hired a flatbed truck and brought the bed through Loughborough town centre to the *Echo*'s office.

"It was a four-poster, steel-framed bed with all kinds of contraptions like cuffs and straps to attach someone to it," Ashe said. "There were two mannequins – one lying on its back, one stood at the head of the bed astride the other." Despite his plea for a racier paper, the editor was shocked by the spectacle unfolding on his doorstep. He told Ashe: "No. Get rid of it. You can't have a sex bed in the car park." The story still made the paper, but the sex-sells experiment had lost its appeal. "After two weeks, we were called in and told 'that's enough sex in the paper'," Ashe said.

Another memorable walk-in came when Manjit Singh – who described himself as Leicestershire's strongest man – arrived to demonstrate his superhuman strength. In the true spirit of local news, Ashe and

Jarram invited Singh to lift each of them off the ground – then to lift them both at the same time. "I spent a happy hour being picked up by him," Ashe recalled. "In fact, I don't think anyone ever had as much fun as we did arranging for things to happen in that car park." Other car-park capers included a visit from a machine that appeared on TV gameshow *Robot Wars*.

While the *Echo*'s car park was apparently the epicentre of the walk-in universe at this time, the team also had a "stuffy, windowless room" for interviews. One visitor to this room explained that sugar was the cause of many of the world's ills – including baldness and a recent red card for footballer Wayne Rooney. "Very rarely did we get to the point of saying we won't run this story," Ashe said. "We didn't do the sugar story, but we were very much for the community. If someone had taken the time to come in, we tried to get at least a couple of lines in the paper."

That view is not shared by every journalist. Plenty of those interviewed for this book said they avoided walk-ins whenever they could. In the case of particularly unwelcome visitors, jumping out of the window (chapter one) or hiding in a cupboard (chapter six) is not unheard of. I tended to sit down with people and get my notebook out – partly because I lacked the backbone to dismiss timewasters, leaving me with little option but to find a story. I was also fascinated by the people who walked in, and their reasons for doing so. Echoing this view, Ashe recalled a walk-in who brought a potato shaped like a seal. He said: "That person has found that potato and thought 'you know who would like that? Isaac at the Echo'."

CHAPTER THREE
Animal, vegetable or mineral? Deadly jam, lucky duck & Nazi greyhound

"Hi guys, there's a man in reception. He says he's grown a pair of really big cucumbers, wants someone to take a look at them."

As soon as I read these words – a response from Alex Wood to my initial tweet about walk-ins – I knew I needed a chapter about prize vegetables and the other flora and fauna that are drawn by some strange magnetism to local newsrooms. Apparently, there's no point growing a record-breaking squash if you can't carry it to the local paper for all to see.

As I discovered in the curious case of Mr Massimo's aubergines, these stories encapsulate both the hilarity and the value of local news. It's often weird and parochial, but local news can give people a platform to celebrate their achievements. In my experience, these people were rarely self-promoters in the modern social-media sense. This was more about sharing their passions than getting clicks and likes. Following the local onion enthusiast wasn't possible until recently, except occasionally in the local paper, and that was probably best for all concerned.

Reporter Alex Wood (right) with one of the giant cucumbers.
Credit: Robin Murray

While green-fingered visitors rarely arrive bearing front-page news, they often provide free home-grown produce. This is usually fine, as long as you can figure out what to do with a carrier bag stuffed with kale. However, sometimes a little journalistic scepticism is still required. David Bishop wisely refused to eat a gift brought to him in the mid-1980s, when he worked as a cadet reporter in a branch office of the *Daily News* in

Hāwera, New Zealand. Bishop was the only reporter in the office when a man in his sixties, with a bomber jacket and a combover, came upstairs from reception.

The man told him: "I need to correct something terrible that was in the gardening page." He went on to explain that the paper was giving deadly nightshade a bad name by suggesting it could be dangerous. He said the plant was in fact perfectly safe to grow in gardens, and added: "I make my own jam out of deadly nightshade berries." The man conceded that "you have to be careful" with the amount of berries you use, and that they are all properly cooked.

But things were about to get worse. Bishop said: "He gets out a jar of this jam, plonks it on the desk and invites me to have a sample." Muttering something about having just eaten, Bishop suggested that the man could leave the jam behind. Thankfully, the man agreed, and contented himself with extolling the virtues of deadly nightshade in various recipes. "He went away feeling much happier," Bishop said.

"I put the deadly nightshade jam in the bin, like a normal person would do," he added. "I'm not a gardening expert, but a clue is probably in the name." More than three decades on, Bishop said he did not regret missing the chance to sample such a rare jam. "I decided I would pass on that particular experience," he said. "Call me old fashioned, but when a jar of jam has the word 'deadly' in large, slightly wobbly handwriting on the label, it doesn't fill me with confidence."

• • •

Potatoes seem like a safer foodstuff than deadly nightshade (cue letters from the nightshade jam lobby), but a reader who walked into reception at the *Salford Advertiser* in Eccles in the mid-1980s wasn't offering a meal. These potatoes were special. Beaming from beneath a flat cap, the man said, "I've got a story for you", then reached into a plastic shopping bag for the proof: three potatoes.

"He produced them one by one," said reporter Nigel Wiskar. Having done so, the man said: "They are a family of ducks." Wiskar squinted and tried to see ducks in the admittedly ill-formed spuds. His conclusion: "Number one, yes. Number two, perhaps. Number three? It's just a small potato, mate."

"I didn't have the heart to say," Wiskar told me. The man was "so chuffed" with his potato ducks that – like many reporters down the years – Wiskar decided his only option was to run the story. He fetched photographer Harry Potts, whose image of the man and his potato ducks says everything about the curious magic of walk-ins.

. . .

In case you're thinking weird walk-ins are unique to the UK and Ireland, or even the wider English-speaking world, think again. Simon Aldra works in the local press in Norway, for title called *Brønnøysunds Avis*. Visitors there have ranged from the sublime to the ridiculously unpleasant.

First, the latter. A local politician was unhappy about something. Aldra can't remember exactly what the man's gripe was, but he thinks the editor refused to publish some of his letters, as they "weren't all that relevant". How did this pillar of the local community react? He filled the paper's letterbox with, as Aldra put it, "literal chicken shit".

In a tale more in keeping with Scandinavia's reputation for polite, resourceful people, Aldra shared a story from 1969 (before his time at the paper) along with a picture of a smartly dressed man holding a fish and a gigantic potato. Aldra explained: "This is Anders from Bindal. He's found a very big potato and quite a rare fish. So he's put on his best suit and coat, driven for a couple of hours and taken the ferry to visit the paper to get his photo taken." The impressive potato weighed almost a kilogramme (more than two pounds), and the (translated) headline could grace any local paper worldwide: "Rare fish and large potato in Bindal."

• • •

The receptionist's tone did not fill Chris Burn with confidence. She simply said a man had brought something to show a reporter. Nothing more. But Burn – then chief reporter at the Shrewsbury branch office of the *Shropshire Star* – said: "There was a note of uncertainty in her voice." The building was small, with reception downstairs and reporters in a little room above. "Normally, we went down to see people in reception, but for whatever reason he came upstairs," Burn said.

The day was hot, and Burn found himself face to face with the man in the cramped, sweltering office. The man seemed intense. He told Burn: "I have got something in this bag that you need to see." Giving no clue about the contents, the man held out the black bin liner – and Burn cautiously peeked inside.

"There were three or four dead bats," he said. "Obviously you don't expect that. I remember managing to keep a straight face." Like many reporters interviewed for this book, Burn felt the safest option was simply to ask some questions – "partly out of nervousness".

"I always think [you should] hear people out because there's a chance there might be something in it," he said. In this case, a story did begin to emerge. Burn continued: "He hadn't killed them. He had found them under a railway bridge."

Burn was aware of repair work being done to Shrewsbury's main railway bridge. The man said he had found the bats beneath the bridge, and seen more floating in the river – apparently killed by some aspect of the works, possibly pressure washing. After Burn promised to look into the story, the man left. "He took his bats with him," Burn said.

The story stood up. Police confirmed they were investigating and, although no criminal charges resulted, the works were temporarily stopped. Burn was told this was a "planned break", but the timing struck him as "convenient". The man with the bats (hereafter Batman) posed for a picture beside the bridge.

"He didn't have his bag of bats in the picture," Burn said, admitting this was a disappointment. "The *Shropshire Star* wasn't that kind of paper." The story ended up on the front page of the *Star*'s Shrewsbury edition, and Burn is glad he met Batman. "It can be hard to filter out time wasters from those who genuinely have a story," he said. "That story was a really good lesson for me to hear people out. I've covered lots of good stories but that's one of the most memorable."

Reflecting on the closure of newspaper offices, Burn said people like Batman might struggle to tell their stories. Seeing a bag of dead bats made him take notice. Trying to explain that over the phone or via email would have been difficult, he said, adding: "You can still get really good stories from Twitter or Facebook. That's a new way of connecting with people, but it's a different audience. There are stories that we're probably all missing out on."

• • •

Jonathan Whiley also used the words "most memorable" to describe the tale of the "Nazi greyhound". It was 2012, and Whiley was a trainee at three weekly papers – the *Merthyr Express*, the *Rhymney Valley Express* and the *Gwent Gazette* – based at an office in Merthyr Tydfil.

"I spent about eighteen months there in all and it was a busy news patch. On my first week in the job, I had to cover a murder investigation, which set the tone," he said: "The office was in the centre of the town, with a wide front desk run by two receptionists and the news desk directly behind – in full view of any member of the public coming in with a story or complaint."

One such visitor was a retired teacher, formerly head of art at a local school, who asked to see a reporter. Whiley took the man into a small side room that was used for interviews, and they "spent a good hour talking it through".

His story was this: in 1941, Hitler's deputy Rudolf Hess flew to Britain to try to broker a peace deal. His plane crashed near Glasgow, but he managed to parachute out and was arrested by a farmer wielding a pitchfork. He was later taken to Maindiff Court Military Hospital in Abergavenny, where he was treated for mental illness. All this was in the historical record – but the teacher also said Hess had been allowed to keep a greyhound, to try to keep his mind off committing suicide. And he said Hess's guards often took the dog (but not the owner) to the local dog track to race on Saturdays.

Whiley did some research and spoke to a local historian, and it turned out the greyhound – called Nimrod – was indeed a regular at the Penydarren Park track during the war. The story ran on page three (the traditional home of quirky tales in the local press) and was picked up by the nationals. "It was a surreal story and one that sticks with me," Whiley said. But it didn't end there.

"A few days after, an elderly woman called into the office to add further detail to the story," Whiley said. The woman said Nimrod's Nazi connection was well known locally. She told Whiley that her father had taken her to watch the greyhounds when she was about eight. She added: "He gave me a sixpenny piece and told me not to tell my mother that he was going to the races and taking me with him. I can remember the greyhounds coming out, and I was told that there was a famous one there – Nimrod. It was a marvellous dog. It was light brown and it had a bit of a streak. I picked him to bet on, and he won, and came up with two shillings and sixpence, which was a small fortune then."

Whiley's time at the Welsh weeklies also included reporting on "the beast of Merthyr Tydfil". He said: "We had several people come into the office and claim that they had seen a big cat – a black panther – roaming the local area. Such were the sightings – a bus driver to a farmer and several residents (one warned it could eat a small child) – that we ran it as a front-page story. It became the talk of the town and we ran follow-ups for weeks."

Pictures of a big cat and the Nazi greyhound (note: the political views of the deceased canine are not known) both featured on Whiley's leaving page (a mock-up front page made as a memento for journalists when they leave a newspaper). It must have been hard to pick a lead for that page, as his other articles included a woman who hit him with a newspaper ("I can't remember for the life of me what the story was") and a man who walked in and announced he had killed his entire family. Whiley explained: "It turns out that this wasn't true – the man was suffering from mental health problems – but at the time, we didn't know and it was a scary situation. He was coaxed outside, the office was locked and we rang the police."

. . .

The issue of mental health came up repeatedly as I researched and wrote this book. I have omitted many stories where the punchline might have been at the expense of someone with mental health issues. The focus here is on journalists, and what it's like to work in local news. However, a book about local news – especially one about walk-ins – inevitably includes highly eccentric characters, and some who were probably unwell. For this reason, I rarely name or give identifiable details of the people journalists encountered. I hope any laughs will relate to the reporters and their predicaments, not the struggles of vulnerable people. I have attempted to deal with all stories sensitively, keeping the focus on the reporters, and making no attempt at amateur diagnosis of mental health disorders.

Keeping that distance is easy when sitting at a desk, writing a book. However, for many of the journalists in this book – including me – this was not always an option. Journalists are sometimes the last resort for desperate people with complex problems that have not been resolved elsewhere – including by health services, social care, councils and the police. Many such visitors demand a story is written. Others simply talk, if a journalist will listen.

During my own time as a journalist, I had no training about mental health, but I often met people who clearly needed professional support and treatment. One simple thing a journalist can do for a vulnerable person is think carefully before publishing anything. A visitor may want to be featured in the paper, but that often struck me as a very bad idea. On the other hand, I was wary of making such judgements on someone else's behalf.

Easier options exist. Where appropriate, I directed people to council or healthcare services. I sometimes contacted these services myself. It's surprising how often a simple call to an organisation's press office sparks action.

To be honest, I never truly cracked this problem. I usually listened and did what I could for people, which wasn't much. Looking back, I know I could have done more. Being young, anxious and ambitious, I focussed on my job – stories, pictures, deadlines. Without sacrificing much time or effort, I could have thought more deeply about the people I met, and tried harder to point them towards help, or brought help to them. At the very least, I should have armed myself with a list of great local services (which I often wrote about) that might have welcomed them.

Chapter seven contains several examples of journalists helping people who others might have ignored. As one reporter puts it, a "bit of heart" goes a long way.

• • •

"When you went to reception, you had to go down three flights of stairs," said Stuart Robinson, who worked for the *Yorkshire Evening Post* in a huge newsroom that also housed the *Yorkshire Post*. "You had that long trudge to think about 'what's waiting for me when I get down there?'" The walk culminated in a long corridor – like a football stadium tunnel – where the reporter could see the "enthusiastic walk-in" waiting at the far end. Robinson said ninety-nine out of a hundred were "not a story", adding: "You'd be thinking 'how long is it going to take me to get rid of them?'"

But in March 2010, a van driver became that one-in-a-hundred visitor. When Robinson reached reception, the driver – a "really nice, down-to-earth guy" – was already speaking to a security guard at reception, and he led the guard and Robinson outside to his van.

"I've got a duck stuck in the engine compartment," he told them. And so he did. He explained that he had startled a flock of ducks on a country road in Belgium, and believed he had hit and killed one. Thinking no more of it, he had driven to Calais, crossed to England on a ferry then driven all the way to Yorkshire before stopping at services and noticing a hole in the radiator grille on the front of the van.

Incredibly, the duck was alive. Robinson recalled wondering "is this for real?" But he had a more pressing problem: the driver and the security guard didn't want to touch the duck – and someone had to get it out.

"The poor little thing is just sitting there in the dark, looking up at me and the security guy and the driver," he said. "I'm a bit of an animal lover. The security guy got some latex gloves and I reached in and gently picked it up." The duck didn't struggle. Robinson put it in a box, and the van driver said he would take it to a local animal charity.

Robinson took some pictures and the driver's phone number, then went back to the office and told his editor: "I think we might have a tale here." The story got national and international coverage – including a report in Belgium about their missing duck, and one in a Canadian town whose ice hockey team had a duck mascot. At the van driver's request, Robinson's write-up included the name of the garage that had fixed the van – because the mechanics said there would be no charge if they got a mention.

Robinson followed up with the animal charity, who said the duck was not injured and had been released in a local park. "It hopefully lived happily ever after. I don't know if there's a language barrier with ducks," he said. "I like to think it's still out there in a local park, quacking in Flemish."

"This walk-in kind of encapsulates that importance of your local paper," said Robinson, who thinks something unquantifiable has been lost with the decline of walk-ins. "People weren't going to the paper because they wanted to be famous or go viral or make money. They genuinely thought that the paper would know what to do because the paper was such a trusted thing in towns and cities." Speaking about the van driver who brought him the duck, he added: "This guy's first thought was to go to the *Evening Post* – 'they'll know what to do'. I think that's the thing with walk-ins. People thought that the paper was this sort of fount of all knowledge."

On working in local journalism, Robinson added: "You will never ever have another job like that. I will always feel incredibly fortunate to have been part of something so unique. It prepares you so much to go on to other stuff because you have worked in a job that no one else has experienced. You've got that bank of experience and that ability just to tip up to work and deal with… whatever your boss throws at you."

Many people interviewed for this book echoed this sentiment. Working life often revolves around routine. In most jobs, workers can build a comfort zone then stay within it. For better or worse, journalism forces you to construct that comfort zone on shifting sand – you simply have to deal with whatever story or deadline comes your way. This gave me skills and confidence I could barely have imagined on the day I arrived at the *Crawley News*. Like me, many of the people featured in this book are no longer journalists – but the resourcefulness and sense of fun acquired in local news lasts a lifetime.

• • •

An unlucky duck was among the odd items brought to *Retford Times* reporter James Peck by a regular visitor called Roy. Roy was in his seventies, with a strong Retford accent and milk-bottle glasses. He still lived with his mum, but at some point he had worked for the *Retford Times*.

"This somehow entitled him, in his mind, to a free copy of the paper every Thursday," Peck said, adding that no one objected. "The receptionists didn't want to speak to him. They sent him straight through to me, but I relished speaking to him because I found him fascinating and very funny." A particular quirk of Roy's routine involved visiting Brigg market – some thirty miles away – before his weekly walk-in at the *Times*. At the market he would buy live ducks, geese or chickens to "neck" at home. "He'd have these live birds in crates in his car when he came to see us," Peck recalled. "He preferred the flavour of a freshly killed bird. Once, he came in with a dead duck in his [large jacket] pocket."

When Peck started work at the *Retford Times* in 2004, the office housed twenty-six staff, including editorial, advertising and production. "By the time I left in 2018, it was just me and a receptionist," he said.

The office is now closed, with the paper largely produced from Lincoln. "That's not even in the same county – Retford is in Nottinghamshire," said Peck. "I am from this town and I loved serving it, but I can't bring myself to read the paper now." He added: "Walk-ins are the heart and soul of what a local paper should be. It's a service." But he said staff cuts, office closures and the rise of social media meant local papers have "lost the ability to be the storytellers".

• • •

Our attitudes to animals are complicated. One man saves a duck, another kills one and shoves it in his pocket. Journalists – especially in local news – have to give everyone a hearing, however strange their views may seem. Sometimes it takes a minute to work out whether someone really means what they're saying (spoiler alert: they almost always do).

David Blackmore remembers this feeling after a woman arrived at the *Dorking and Leatherhead Advertiser*, apparently devastated about the death of a squirrel. "It was one of those when you think 'is she just having us on?'" he said. Far from it. The woman was deadly serious, and soon the whole town shared her grief. You see, Albi was no ordinary squirrel. A pure-white albino, he lived in and around a town-centre churchyard, and had become a popular feature of local life.

Now he had been run over. The woman had seen it happen. Recognising the seriousness of the situation – and the chance of a front-page story in this peaceful patch – Blackmore headed to the scene. Getting quotes was easy, but there was a problem: pictures. The paper could hardly use a photo of a squashed squirrel. They had images of Albi in life, but they needed something more.

Blackmore suggested laying some flowers. A colleague added an "awful poem", written at deadline speed to place at the roadside. Good thinking. This gave them something to photograph. But soon the picture changed. The flowers "multiplied", Blackmore said. Seeing the Advertiser's bouquet, local people began adding their own, and soon an impressive floral tribute lay at the fatal spot.

"It was almost generating our own news in a sense," Blackmore said. And it didn't stop there. National papers picked up the story, followed by *Fox News* and *Have I Got News For You*. Without the walk-in, Blackmore said none of this would have happened. He had not appreciated the outpouring of grief that would greet Albi's demise – but he soon understood

Albi's importance to the town, and wrote a story under the headline: "Tears for dead squirrel."

· · ·

As news editor at the *Advertiser* from 2010-13, just after Blackmore's time there, I can identify with the need to generate news. In some places, "hard news" (crime, death and destruction) is easy to find. Happily for the people of peaceful, prosperous Dorking, hard news is rare. But all newspapers need a front-page story (AKA a "splash") and eye-catching lead stories for the first few pages. So, while my fellow news editors on the fringes of London could often file hard news to our shared pool of sub-editors (by then located in Essex), I often lacked an obvious splash.

One option is simply to file the best story you have, then wait for the subs to phone and say: "This can't be the best story you have." They always knew the answer, of course, but sub-editors are professional pedants (not intended as an insult, but a good sub needs to find the devil in the detail). However, to improve the paper and limit the need for these conversations, we worked hard to generate stories by any means we could think of. We studied local crime statistics, attended countless meetings, called every contact in quiet weeks, manned the *Advertiser* stall at local events, and submitted Freedom of Information Act requests to find out what the council spent on biscuits.

In one entirely self-generated story, we surveyed a hundred random people and created a picture of the "average" local person. What did they wear? Who did they vote for? What football team did they support? The answers weren't wildly surprising, but it gave us a funny front page and saved our readers from yet another splash about car parking.

• • •

Blackmore was working in that same Dorking office when a man walked in holding a small piece of paper. Looking shocked, he said: "Yeah, I've just won the lottery."

"No one really knew how to react," Blackmore said. The man wanted to share the news – and some of his £26 million jackpot. After confirming the win was genuine, the paper published a story. Unsurprisingly, the man's stated intention to hand out cash sparked a huge response. Blackmore recalled a day soon after the story was published when the paper received three full sacks of letters. People had written to the paper, asking for their letters to be passed on to the lottery winner.

A great walk-in can feel like winning the lottery but, like Blackmore, part of you is usually wondering: *Is this real? Can I trust this person?* As we'll see in the next chapter, it's often difficult to be sure.

CHAPTER FOUR
Too good to be true? Bin Laden in Skegness

"Find killer of our sacred swans now!"

This intriguing note – scrawled in pink highlighter – reached me at the *Dorking and Leatherhead Advertiser* in 2011. Sounds like a great story, but I had questions. I looked on the back. Nothing. We asked around, to see if our contacts knew of any swan killings in the area. Nothing. We asked a local animal charity, the police, councillors. Nope. Given the lack of crime in Dorking, a serial swan killer would have been quite a drama. But we never stood the story up. Either the Dorking Swan Murderer remains at large, or no such killer existed.

Much as we wanted more information on this tip-off, I suspect a conversation with the note-writer would have left us disappointed. Indeed, many walk-ins left me wishing the visitor had written a note that I could have quietly slipped into the recycling. More often, people turn up with their unbelievable tales and demand that you run a story. Saying no can be difficult, because being disbelieved hurts. It's part of basic training for police officers, social workers and many others to make people feel heard and believed. That's a reasonable approach for journalists too, but – like people in those other professions – you can't make rash promises. Journalists have an advantage here, too. You've got a pen, paper and (usually) shorthand. Scribbling notes can provide valuable thinking time. You listen, ask questions and keep an open mind. Most people tell the truth, a few are confused or mistaken, and occasionally someone deliberately lies (a few truth twisters will feature in this chapter).

Regardless of whether a journalist has sound professional or legal reasons for refusing to run a story, people often get angry at this perceived rejection. As news editor of the *Advertiser*, I turned down a man's story and he wrote me a letter that began: "Dear shithead". Another woman was so outraged that she scrawled the following note for me to sign: "I am not interested in news because I never challenge authority." When I politely declined to add my signature, she told me to tell my parents I was a "total disgrace as a reporter and a human being". Mum and Dad enjoyed that.

Deciding whether to believe someone isn't the only consideration in journalists' minds, but it's the fundamental first step towards running a story. It's not easy. It depends on a mix of fact-checking, instinct and simply assessing what the person says. If they say they've found King Arthur's skeleton in their back garden, you might need expert verification. If they claim they're running a charity bake sale, you can probably believe them. If someone has no obvious reason to lie, they're probably telling the truth. Right?

Not necessarily, as Paul Foster can testify. Soon after joining the *Portsmouth News* in 2003, Foster was working in the Gosport office when reception called to say someone was downstairs. The visitor was an eighteen-year-old woman, who told Foster she had been walking in a rougher part of Gosport when she felt a pain in her leg, and realised she had been shot with an air rifle.

"She rolled up her trousers and showed me the wound, which was just above the knee," Foster said. The woman seemed credible and – after police confirmed they were investigating – Foster had no qualms about writing the story, which was published along with a picture of the woman and her leg wound.

A nineteen-year-old man then came forward with a similar story. He had been shot in the same road, just forty-eight hours later. The *News* reported this too, writing that the man had fallen victim to a "sniper terrorising an estate". One of the man's friends said he had caught a glimpse of a person dressed in black clothing running away. Police carried out door-to-door inquiries, trying to locate this mysterious, leg-obsessed sharpshooter. For a while, nothing happened. No one else was shot, and police didn't catch the sniper. Foster made a diary note to check on the story, and thought nothing more of it.

But when he made that follow-up call to the police, they gave him some surprising news: the victims had made it all up. Not unreasonably, Foster pointed out that the woman had showed him the wound on her leg. The wound was indeed real, the police explained, but the circumstances were a work of (extremely odd) fiction.

"She had been shot on purpose by her boyfriend," Foster said, still somewhat baffled two decades on. "It was a *Shameless*-style plot to try and get money and sympathy from the local community. The idea was to have an outpouring of sympathy, and for some reason they thought they would get a boatload of cash." The woman had not asked Foster to mention anything about money in his story, and it's unclear how the money-making scheme was supposed to work.

Reporting the pair's arrest on suspicion of perverting the course of justice, the *News* said they had hoped to "claim government compensation of at least £1,000".

Foster is uncertain on how the police unravelled the bizarre plot, but thinks the "victims" may have backed out and changed their stories. "I think it's the only time that I had someone lie so convincingly," added Foster, who now teaches journalism. "I tell that story to my students to give them an example that people will sometimes lie directly to your face."

While Foster's example is extreme, it raises a broader question about why people want their stories printed. One reason is trust in local papers. By getting their weird conspiracy published, Foster's clumsy fraudsters thought people would believe it. In my time as news editor of the *Dorking and Leatherhead Advertiser*, I was acutely aware of the paper's long history and position in the community. When people asked us to print a story, they wanted our seal of approval – proof that something happened, and that it mattered.

Foster said the closure of newspaper offices "affects this brand recognition", which "can impact on trust in local journalists". A 2021 UK poll found that 58% of people would trust a local news organisation based in the area it reported on, while only 31% would trust one based outside the area. Foster said a local presence shows readers the paper and its staff are "part of that community... part of you". He added: "That's the element that has been lost. The community trust will be limited by ripping reporters out of that community. The reader is taking a risk by trusting you. Should they do that if they don't know who you are or what you stand for?"

• • •

Lee Marlow was a regional journalist for twenty-three years, mostly at the *Leicester Mercury*. After so long in the job, stories rarely surprised him – but a strange tale from 2015 sticks in his memory. It wasn't a walk-in. He heard about it at home, during a conversation with his wife, who worked at a local school. A young athlete had visited the school and spoken to the pupils. The athlete was a former hockey player who had broken her back and been paralysed from the waist down. Four years on, she was a canoeist and was aiming to compete at the 2016 Paralympic Games in Rio de Janeiro.

"I got her number and arranged to interview her," Marlow said. "I thought it would be a nice, if standard, 'triumph in the face of adversity' feature for our weekend magazine. I met her, and she was great, interesting, her story was strong. Good quotes. I got on with her. I followed her on Twitter. She followed me. It was all peachy. But there was one line in the piece that didn't quite scan."

The athlete complained about the treatment she had received in hospital after injuring her spine. "She didn't go in to too much detail but she said, repeatedly, that they treated her terribly," Marlow said. "I thought if I was going to include that, I should contact the hospital. The hospital came back a day later and said they kicked her out because she wasn't really paralysed. It wasn't a back or leg injury. It was all in her head." Marlow said he vividly remembers this conversation with the hospital. "My blood ran cold," he said.

He went to his editor, who simply said: "Oh my God." Numerous conversations followed, with Marlow and his colleagues trying to decide what to do and how to approach the story. "What we decided is that this goes to the heart of sport," he said. "She had effectively cheated."

The first step was putting the story to the athlete, which Marlow called "one of the most awkward conversations in my journalistic career… she took it badly, of course". There followed a fraught process of building a fair, accurate and legally watertight story. Rewriting his initial feature from top to bottom,

Marlow aimed to "bring the reader into my seat", breaking it down into chapters. He said he had sleepless nights worrying about every detail of the story, and about the effect on the woman involved. But after all the deliberations, his guiding principle was: "Just tell the truth".

It took "days and days and days" to finish. Then came the scary moment of publication. "The ramifications were huge," Marlow said. The story went national, and the athlete was kicked out of the Paralympics team. Unsurprisingly – she was angry. "She hated us for it," Marlow said. "But it was right we did it."

Later that year, Marlow won feature writer of the year at the Society of Editors Regional Press Awards. "I think it was mainly because of that piece," he said. "It was a strong, original story and I like to think we handled it well."

The story about the athlete had given him a new zest for journalism, but a week after winning the award – for the third year running – there was a twist in Marlow's own story. He said: "The editor called me in. I thought he might want to give me a pay rise. He made me redundant. It seemed to sum up life in regional newspapers in 2016."

Marlow also shared a walk-in story from earlier in

his career, and in this case establishing the truth was painfully easy. The visitor in question, who wanted to be called Lord Luvaduck, said he had found a gold bar. Marlow said the man "reached into his plastic bag and pulled out a house brick sprayed gold".

• • •

"I know where the body is." That's what the man said.

Rob Dex was stunned. But things quickly became even more troubling. "He was an old chap, in his sixties or seventies, hunched over and spoke with a strong local accent which still took me a while to understand, so it was a few seconds before I realised what he was saying," Dex recalled. "I'm pretty sure my mind went totally blank when he lifted his head up and I saw his face with bloody streaks down both cheeks and dried blood all over his neck and on his hands."

Let's rewind a little. It was 2001, and reception had called to say someone wanted to talk to a reporter about a murder. Dex, then a trainee at the *Cornish Guardian*'s St Austell office, had eagerly volunteered. He said: "My two vastly more experienced colleagues were suppressing giggles as I bounded down the two flights of stairs. I knew it was probably nothing, but I also knew there is always a chance of a big story falling into your lap."

"I know where they put the little girl," the walk-in said. "Genette Tate. I know where she is." Dex was not from the area, but he said: "Even as an incomer, I knew who Genette Tate was." He added: "She had disappeared in 1978, aged thirteen, from her home over the border in Devon but the case had gripped the whole West Country, and regular appeals were made for information even then." Tate has never been found, so – if true – the walk-in's claim was huge.

Unsure what to think, Dex took notes and contact details and promised to call the man back. He added: "My fearless commitment to journalism did not extend as far as accepting his invitation to accompany him back to his home in one of the outlying villages where he promised to tell me more." They parted ways, and Dex went back upstairs to tell his veteran colleagues all about it.

One of them called a contact – a local councillor – in the village where the man lived, and the mystery was solved within a day. Dex explained: "The old man's wife had died recently. He wasn't always able to look after himself. He didn't always know where he was – or who he was. The councillor would drop by and see him, and see what could be done to help."

Dex added: "It's always stayed with me because it

sums up what is lost now, with the days of solid weeklies and high-street offices almost over. It is not just stories that are lost, but so is the informal support network that meant an old man – whose mind wandered and whose hands shook so much he would cut himself shaving – was looked out for."

• • •

Having trained in Cornwall, Scott Jones might also have worked at the *Cornish Guardian* – but he was delighted to land a job at his hometown paper, the *Coventry Evening Telegraph*. The paper sold about 80,000 copies daily and had a staff including about 40 reporters and 10 sub-editors – numbers unimaginable in local or regional news today. The office was right in the centre of Coventry, in a sea of 1950s and '60s architecture, built after the city was heavily bombed during World War Two.

The location was great for walk-ins, with visitors entering through double glass doors to find a polished marble floor and an enormous wooden counter – 50 or 60 feet long – staffed by a team including receptionists and advertising sales people. A large office on the first floor contained the editorial staff, including business, politics, health and crime desks – so there was no shortage of journalists if a story broke.

"We did a really good job of being on the scene," Jones said. Coventry was a "rough place", he added, with plenty of crime and a wealth of other strong stories for a young journalist to find. But not every story got printed. First, reporters had to pitch their ideas to news editor Peter Mitchell, a "big guy with thick black hair, brushed back, and a big, thick moustache". Mitchell would lean back in his chair, holding a pencil between his moustached top lip and his nose. When a reporter approached and said they had a good story, Mitchell would reply: "I'll be the judge of that."

The *Evening Telegraph* took on two trainee reporters each year, and certain tasks traditionally fell to these newbies. For example, one or the other had to sit in the corner of the newsroom once every hour, pressing their ear to a radio to hear local news bulletins to check the *Evening Telegraph* hadn't missed any important stories. The trainees were also expected to deal with walk-ins.

Jones admits he was sceptical when it came to walk-ins, which were often a waste of time. So he can't remember why, in 1998 – three years into the job and no longer a new trainee – he found himself heading to reception to deal with one.

"I went down to the foyer and there was a guy there who was just sitting patiently in the front window," he said. Jones introduced himself and sat down, and the man began telling the story of his "crazy" experiences since losing his job as a quality controller for car manufacturer Peugeot. Thousands of people had lost jobs due to car factory closures, but this man had responded in a surprising way.

"He didn't know what to do with himself in Coventry if there was no car industry for him," Jones said. The man and his partner had packed their bags and moved to Los Angeles to "see what happens". At first, nothing happened. They struggled to find work, and for a few months it seemed their American dream would end in failure. But one night in a bar, he got chatting to a film industry worker who bemoaned the lack of quality control in Hollywood scriptwriting.

Picking up on two vital words, the former Peugeot worker said: "The only thing I know is quality control." Incredibly, he was told "you're just the man I need" – and in days his life had "turned around". He quickly found himself working in Hollywood studios, where he introduced a quality control system for scripts. Or so he claimed.

Looking at the small, unassuming man, Jones didn't know what to think. Could this be true? The man kept talking, explaining how he had met every Hollywood star and attended exclusive parties – becoming "everyone's mate" in the process. He reeled off a list of famous names.

"You're telling me you're their mate?" Jones asked.

"Yes, that's basically what I'm telling you," the man replied.

Perhaps thinking of the sceptical news editor upstairs, Jones said: "Prove it." The man, who was back in Coventry to visit his mum, said he had evidence at her house, and set off to get it.

"He was back within an hour and he literally had a stack of all the photos," Jones said. The pictures showed the man with a host of Hollywood stars, at "swanky gardens and swimming pools". Jones concluded: "It was obviously all true. I then interviewed him properly about his story." The tale passed the Peter Mitchell Test and appeared in print.

A couple of weeks later, a brown envelope arrived at the *Evening Telegraph* with Jones's name on it. It contained a photo of the actor Nicolas Cage, with a letter from Cage thanking Jones for the excellent story about his friend. Writing on the photo, Cage described Jones as an "ace journalist on the CET" (*Coventry Evening Telegraph*).

Too much trust can get a journalist in trouble – but what about too much suspicion? Looking back on one incident in her career, Dhruti Shah wishes she had been more trusting. It was the mid-2000s, and Shah worked for the *Harrow Observer* in north-west London. Her patch, Pinner, was home to the actor David Suchet, and one day she heard he was leaving the area. Being new and "hungry for stories", Shah dropped a letter at his house, asking for an interview.

She received no reply and, assuming this meant no, it faded from her memory. Work was busy, and being part of the *Observer*'s small, young team left no time to dwell. "We would make jokes and have fun with each other, and there was one guy at the paper who would often make prank calls [to colleagues]," Shah said.

One day, she answered the phone and a voice said: "Hello, this is David Suchet."

Shah replied: "As if". She put the phone down, half amused and half annoyed at her colleague for wasting her time.

The phone rang again. When challenged about this being a prank, the caller said: "I don't know what you're talking about." It doesn't take Hercule Poirot to see where this story is going – it was indeed David (now Sir David) Suchet calling to decline Shah's offer of an interview.

• • •

Celebrities are tricky for local papers. When famous people visit, they're often promoting a book or a show – and you find yourself asking aimless questions about your area to generate a local angle. "Our own" celebrities – the ones who genuinely call your patch home – can only feature in the paper so many times, and the very famous ones often prefer to keep a low local profile.

Things can be even trickier if the celebrity in question isn't a fan of the local paper. In the early 1990s, a proud mother walked into the *Royston Crow* with a story of achievement about her daughter, who was in the early stages of an acting career. The reporters weren't keen.

"My colleague and I dismissed it as a woman blowing her daughter's trumpet too hard, and never followed up," said Martin Tooth. "But we never forgot the daughter's name. So, we were somewhat embarrassed when in 2006 Rachel Weisz won an Oscar. My then former colleague texted me on the day it happened with 'There's a woman in reception with an

Oscar'."

Tooth said he often wondered "if the *Royston Crow* tried to contact Rachel Weisz when she became famous and found it somewhat difficult". I asked this question to Duncan Sandes – a reporter at the *Crow* after Tooth's time – who confirmed that the paper never, in his stint at least, secured an interview with the Hollywood star.

• • •

If the Oscars added a category for "most famous person turned away by a local newspaper" (which, I admit, seems fairly unlikely), the *Leigh Journal* would certainly be in the running. The incident in question happened in the early 1960s and involved reporter Harold Williams, who has since died.

"Harold used to tell the tale with relish," said his former colleague Steve Simpson. It began with a "well-dressed fellow" coming to the counter to tell Williams an exciting new band would soon perform at the Leigh Casino. Williams "listened carefully and sent the man on his way politely", Simpson said. In retrospect, the band in question was probably worth a nib at the very least. Simpson explained that the well-dressed visitor was Brian Epstein and the band – then unknown –

were called the Beatles. "Still part of *Leigh Journal* folklore," he added.

• • •

Any reporter could reject a story about someone who later becomes a global celebrity. But for Rebecca Brice, this wasn't the problem. Picking up the phone at *BBC Radio Lincolnshire*, she received a tip-off about someone extremely famous. Notorious, in fact. The most wanted man on Earth. Trouble was, the story seemed literally unbelievable.

It was the mid-2000s, and Brice was on her first contract at the radio station. Being the newbie meant doing terrible late shifts and locking up the station's creepy building, she said. On one such shift, a woman phoned and told her: "I've got really, really strong evidence to suggest that Osama Bin Laden is living in Skegness."

OK. Now what? Put the phone down? Call the CIA?

Being about five months into the job, Brice was aware of regulars who would call or walk in with bizarre stories. This lady was one of them so – combined with the incredible claims she was making – Brice was extremely sceptical. But, like all good walk-ins (or in this case ring-ins), the woman ploughed on with her story, saying she had sightings and a profile of the al-Qaeda founder – who at that time was being hunted by the US military for his role in the 9/11 terrorist attacks.

Brice admits she didn't know what to do with this situation. She recalls writing notes, then wondering what her colleagues might think if they read them. Deciding not to clear the airwaves to report this world exclusive, she waited until the next morning to speak to her news editor.

"Oh, the Osama Bin Laden lady?" he replied. "Don't waste your time." As it turned out, the lady had walked in previously with a dossier of evidence, keen for coverage of her pet theory.

With the benefit of hindsight (Bin Laden was killed in Pakistan in 2011) it seems unlikely the town that gave us the very first Butlin's resort was also chosen as a hiding place by a fugitive militant leader. However, Brice perfectly described the tiny but persistent doubt that haunts every reporter who dismisses such a story. As she put it on Twitter: "I knew it was absurd but there's always that slight niggle 'what if he IS'!"

That story – and this chapter – should have ended there. But these bizarre tales rarely conclude so neatly. Taking her news editor's advice, Brice forgot the Bin Laden lady and moved on. But the tale came flooding back when she was sent to an incident in Sleaford, following reports that police had found bomb-making equipment. This was a time of heightened terrorism fears. Had al-Qaeda's elusive leader been hiding in Lincolnshire all along? Had she dismissed the story of the century?

Brice was ten minutes from the scene when the office called and told her to stand down. Turns out the model airplane club had crashed some planes, and somehow the pieces had been mistaken for bomb parts.

・ ・ ・

When a homeless man visited the *Surrey Daily Advertiser* in Guildford in the early 1980s, Alan Jones thought he could help. The man was partially sighted, and Jones had been running stories about the lack of accommodation for disadvantaged groups in Guildford. He headed for reception, thinking this might be a front-page story.

"The man was indeed almost blind, and told me his story about the lack of sympathy from the housing department," Jones said. "I told him to sit down while I called the council, from a phone on the reception desk so he could hear my rage." Here is Jones's account of the conversation:

Jones: "Hi, it's Alan Jones, chief reporter of the Surrey Ad here. A man has just walked into our reception complaining you are ignoring his pleas for accommodation. It's outrageous."

Housing officer: "Can you describe him?"

Jones: "He's late fifties, obviously wearing second-hand clothes, long hair, he has a white walking stick. Oh, and appears to have a glass eye."

Housing officer: "Ah, it's him again. He's been claiming disability benefit fraudulently... Has he taken out his glass eye yet and bounced it on the floor? It's something he does when he doesn't get his own way."

Jones: "Er, OK..."

Jones to homeless man: "I'm afraid there's nothing the council can do. I can point you to a homeless charity in the town who might be able to help you."

Homeless man: "You don't believe I'm nearly blind, do you?" [removes glass eye and bounces it on the floor, to screams from the receptionists].

"It took a while to find his eye, give it back to him... and send him on his way," Jones said. "I didn't answer calls from reception for a while after that."

• • •

"In 2003, I had a walk-in of someone who claimed in all seriousness to have witnessed the Columbia space shuttle disaster from north London," said Martin Beckford, then of the *Enfield Gazette*. Given that the shuttle was destroyed over Texas in the USA, this tale seemed unlikely. Still, like many good walk-ins, the man had evidence. "He had taken a photo and printed it out and it was just a picture of the sky with some clouds," Beckford explained. "He was adamant that you could see the space shuttle blow up." The man, who had come in with his son, seemed perfectly calm and rational, leaving the paper's staff confused about his motives. "Afterwards, we just couldn't be sure whether he genuinely thought it, or he just did it as a joke," Beckford said.

The *Gazette* refused to publish the empty-sky picture, but on another occasion a cheeky local sneaked a joke into its pages. For reasons that still baffle Beckford, the paper used to run a weekly vox pop in local pubs, with patrons giving their views on issues of the day. One week, a young person on work experience came back with a quote – that was duly printed in the paper – from a Mr Billy Sollocks.

Experiences like these have left Beckford unsure about the pros and cons of dealing with local characters. He said: "Our rival paper, the *Enfield Independent*, had its office right next to a bus stop in the town centre so they got way more walk-ins than we did. Not sure whether that was good or bad." Beckford said many readers see their local paper as a public service that is duty-bound to run their stories, and that anyone who has not worked in journalism "wouldn't believe some of the weird ideas that people would contact the local paper with" (see almost every page of this book).

"The local paper was the only outlet for a long time, pre internet," Beckford added. "It was the only way that people could feel like their stories were being heard." The internet age – especially social media – has weakened local journalism by providing both new sources of information and new ways for people to share their stories. Some of the impacts have been positive, but (as mentioned earlier in this chapter, and discussed in more detail later) social media lacks the credibility of quality journalism. On social media, you have to make your own judgements about what to believe. In the local paper, reporters and editors should have done that tricky work for you – and simply refused to print stories that don't "stand up" (to stand up a story means finding sufficient evidence to print or broadcast it).

However, as this chapter shows, far-fetched stories can be true, while other (apparently more believable) tales may be false. One conclusion is that journalists can't win. Not every fact can be checked. Sometimes you simply have to make a judgement. You get a little protection by quoting people – making it clear this is what they said, rather than a statement of fact by the reporter. But ultimately you lend someone your credibility by running their story. There's no silver bullet here, no single answer. However, journalists are intelligent, resourceful, nosy people who specialise in people. The deceptions included in this chapter stuck in reporters' minds because they were outliers.

One other point should be made – one that ought not to be controversial: most journalists are honest. Bear with me here. If you're feeling an urge to yell "fake news" and hurl this book across the room, take a breath. Journalism is finding stuff out and reporting it to your audience. At the very top, in the 24/7 chaos of national and international news, a class of self-promoting commentators have muscled in wearing big "I'm a journalist" badges. Their news-as-entertainment model, which works by generating outrage, hasn't helped us. It hasn't helped our politics and society, it hasn't helped inform the public, and it has sullied the reputation of journalists.

Alongside this breed of faux journalists (many of whom are really politicians or lobbyists), a far greater number of national news reporters struggle to report the news. With many stories distorted by comment before the facts are established, reporting the facts becomes controversial. I covered UK news for the BBC website from 2012 to 2016 (the run-up to, and aftermath of, the Brexit referendum). Our team tried to report the facts, and I never heard colleagues express support for either side in the referendum. But the commentator "journalists" drowned us out. False outrage about bendy bananas got more clicks than sober judgements and plain old facts.

Happily for local journalists, stories they cover are rarely poisoned in this way. The outrage industry is usually too busy with national news. Also, while national papers cater to ideological groups (consider a *Mail* reader, a *Guardian* reader, etc) local papers need to attract a broad audience in their area. Some local papers have a broadsheet (serious) or tabloid (sensational) slant, but it wouldn't make sense business-wise to aim for a niche political group. As a result, proper local journalists – trained, qualified professionals, not to be confused with bloggers, influencers or prolific

Facebook posters – retain a unique role. This has declined as budgets, staff numbers, offices and readership have declined, but it's not gone.

In my experience, the vast majority of local reporters do the job with enthusiasm, honesty and integrity. I was inspired by my conversations with all the wonderful journalists who feature in this book, especially those still working today. That dedication to honest reporting is not 100% effective at weeding out fake news, but it's the best available option. A few rogue stories will always slip through, even with the most watertight set of editorial policies. Martin Beckford shared a simpler idea – an inviolable rule from the *Enfield Gazette* that (arguably) spared readers just as much pain: "No poems."

CHAPTER FIVE

The walking dead: Mortality mix-ups

IN 2015, DURING MY TIME AT THE BBC, one of my colleagues killed the Queen. Sort of. At least, that's how some newspapers reported it. Specifically, they said she "killed off" the Queen by mistakenly announcing her death (seven years before it actually happened). For anyone not familiar with the beyond-parody workings of our beloved broadcasting corporation, the BBC periodically conducts rehearsals for royal deaths. This always baffled me. Our day job was to report the news, and we were perfectly familiar with reporting the deaths of famous people – the golden rule being: don't say someone's dead until you're sure. I realise the death of a major royal – a *Category One*, in BBC speak – is a big deal, and the BBC needs to get it right. But having a special, complicated process seems like an excellent way to screw it up.

In the case mentioned above, a *BBC Urdu* reporter – who had not been told a royal death rehearsal was taking place – saw an internal monitor displaying the news, and shared it on Twitter. The BBC Trust later called it a "grave error of judgement". Leaving aside this incredible – and presumably accidental – pun, I'd say at least some of the error belonged to the organisation rather than the individual. Journalists like sharing news, and seeing this story apparently broadcast on BBC TV seemed like strong enough confirmation to the reporter. As well as facing disciplinary action, the reporter made international headlines. When the *Evening Standard* door-knocked her, a relative told them: "She is not here. She just made a mistake." It must have been a terrible time for her but – when it comes to grave errors – she's in good company.

• • •

One Friday morning in spring 2013, Harry Walsh sat at his desk at the *Donegal News*. The paper was out that day, carrying front-page news of a murder – a rare occurrence in the paper's peaceful patch. The office was quiet, but any hope of a post-deadline lull was about to shatter.

"The receptionist appeared, asking for someone to speak to a man in reception," Walsh recalled. "I was the only reporter in the office, so I went to see what was going on."

He found himself facing an agitated couple. The man was especially angry, yelling in Polish and banging the counter behind which Walsh stood.

"The woman spoke a little English, and she said we had the wrong man on the front page," Walsh said. "I could see that. The murder victim we had pictured was standing in front of me."

Catching the drift of the yelling, Walsh realised the man in reception was actually the victim's brother. Walsh had not written the story himself, but that hardly mattered. He was, in his words, totally helpless.

"What can you do in that situation? You just have to say sorry," he said. "My style is to put my hands up if I've made a mistake. You just have to do what you can to rectify it. He was obviously upset but he couldn't say it in English, which made things harder. He spent half an hour cursing, but I calmed him down and said we would print an apology."

Explaining how the mix-up happened, Walsh told me the paper had been given a picture of five men, including two brothers, and the wrong brother had been pointed out as the dead man.

"It was a bad situation. The man was dealing with his brother's death and then our mistake as well," he said.

Walsh recalled another mix-up, also involving a pair of brothers, during his early days at the paper in 1990.

"One of my jobs then was to keep an eye on local deaths," he said. "I had to call the local undertaker, and one day he gave me all the details of a man that had died. I wrote it up and it appeared in the paper."

On the Friday the story was published, Walsh was called to reception and found the man's widow. Or, rather, the woman who would have been his widow – if he had been dead.

"She said her husband was sitting eating his cornflakes that day and found himself reading his own obituary," Walsh said. He soon discovered that the undertaker had given him the name of the wrong brother. "My editor came out and took the lady and myself into his office. The lady was upset and shocked, but she was very polite. The editor explained it and she accepted the explanation. Once she was calm, he asked her, 'By the way, how does it read?'"

. . .

Harry Walsh's tale of dead men walking sounds like a journalist's worst nightmare, but Dan Slee might beg to differ. Like Walsh, Slee's tale begins on a Friday – some ten years later, in the early 2000s. He was on call at the Sandwell office of the *Express & Star*. While checking the police voicebank for stories, he heard that a woman in her sixties had been killed by a lorry in Wednesbury, a few miles away.

"The police had released the name and the age and that was it," he said.

This being the early days of the internet, Slee scoured a copy of the electoral roll that was kept in the office (he asked me not to use the woman's real name, so I'll call her Jane Jones). A few Jane Joneses appeared on the list, so he rushed out and went door to door. Each encounter began with an awkward moment in which Slee had to ask, in subtle terms: "Did the dead Jane Jones live here?"

He couldn't find the right house. Every Jane Jones appeared to be alive and well. Meanwhile, the news desk in Wolverhampton sent over a picture of a Jane Jones, and Slee was told to take it out and get confirmation that it showed the woman who had died.

"I got back to the office and the evening's paper had come out with the photo on the front," he said. Slee was surprised, but he supposed a colleague must have got the identity confirmed. In fact, no one had. They had simply taken what Slee called a stab in the dark.

"The full story of what had happened never actually got back to us," he said. What did come back, however, was an unhappy update: the woman pictured on the front page was not the Jane Jones who had died. Again, messages from HQ did not explain how this had been discovered. Slee was simply told: "This is the wrong photo. Could you find both families?"

So, having tried and failed to find the family of Jane Jones (deceased), Slee now spent his Friday night searching Wednesbury for that family and Jane Jones (alive), whose picture had been wrongly published along with a story about her namesake's death. Slee stayed out until 10pm, checking in with the news desk every half hour. Still finding none of the relevant Joneses, he went home, then resumed the search on Saturday morning.

It ended with a phone call from the office: where Jane Jones (alive) and the family of Jane Jones (deceased) had both arrived. Happily for Slee, he got back to the office to find his colleague Nina Davies dealing with the families. He described Davies as a "lovely person, full of empathy", adding: "If you could pick anybody to sort someone else's fuck up, it would be Nina."

Feeling that his name might be in the frame for this particular error – despite his innocence – Slee said he entered the office rather sheepishly, to find Davies deep in conversation with assorted Joneses. He caught Davies' eye, to see if she needed any help, but everything seemed to be under control.

He went upstairs to the editorial floor. When Davies came up a while later, she said she had pacified both families. Slee does not recall what the paper did – possibly a combination of an apology and a tribute to Jane Jones (deceased) – but his experiences on that Friday and Saturday are seared into his brain.

Slee never heard who made the mistake or what punishment, if any, they received. This was puzzling, because he said the *Express & Star*'s reputation at this time was: "One strike and you're out." He said the "Sword of Damocles" hung over every reporter, adding: "If anyone made a mistake, they were sent to Ice Station Zebra" – a particular district office that housed out-of-favour staff.

"It wasn't the most nurturing environment as a newspaper, but the district office in Sandwell was marvellous," Slee said. "Ken and Dave [two veteran reporters] knew exactly what to tell the news desk and what not to tell the news desk."

• • •

While Dan Slee's weekend with the Joneses sticks in his memory, Nina Davies – the colleague who smoothed it all over – says she barely remembers it. This perhaps reflects every journalist's ability to remember their own horror stories, while only retaining a vague recollection of other people's.

In her case, the "almighty mistake" that stays with her occurred during her first reporting job, at the *Shrewsbury Chronicle*. Her duties included the wedding and funeral announcements, and one day she finished these and went home, thinking everything was fine. No one noticed anything was wrong until the weekly paper came out.

Davies remembered writing about a wedding at Shrewsbury's Lord Hill Hotel, with a honeymoon in the Dominican Republic to follow. But she hadn't written honeymoon. She had written funeral: the wedding would be followed by a *funeral* in the Dominican Republic. It was picked up by *BBC Radio Shropshire* – with jokes about *Four Weddings and a Funeral* – but Davies did not listen to the radio that Thursday morning, so she arrived at work unaware of her error.

"I walked in to ashen faces on everyone," she said. "No one really looked me in the eye. I got called in by the chief reporter and asked for an explanation. He threw the report at me. I was just utterly gobsmacked." Before she had time to consider how the error had happened, Davies found herself having to phone the family to apologise.

"I can still see the room I was in and the desk I sat at when I had to make the call," she said. "She [the bride] was the most lovely lady." On hearing that the wedding report was in the paper, the lady said: "That's fantastic. We've been wondering when it would go in." Davies struggled to get her next words out, but finally explained the honeymoon-funeral faux pas.

"There was just silence at the other end of the phone," she said. "Then she fell about laughing." Relieved at this reaction – and promising a correction in the next week's paper – Davies put down the phone, but found the mood in the office remained mirthless. She apologised to the chief reporter, and they went to see their editor – who "read the Riot Act".

When Davies told them about the family's reaction, the atmosphere finally began to soften, and the chief reporter started rubbing his big moustache – apparently trying not to laugh. Davies and the chief reporter left the editor's office together, at which point the chief reporter gave her a surprising piece of information.

The editor had subbed (edited) the wedding announcement, and had picked up a mistake in the spelling of Dominican – but he hadn't noticed the claim that the Caribbean nation would host a post-wedding funeral. Everyone makes mistakes.

* * *

In spring 1982, as a "newly minted trainee" on the *South Wales Echo*, Iain McBride found himself on the bottom rung of the newsroom ladder.

"In that humble role it was made clear that, despite passing the first stages of the NCTJ exams, we 'knew nothing' and – even worse – as graduates we had to prove we were streetwise and not 'academic'," he recalled. Based in Cardiff city centre, he tried to find a story in every walk-in – but it wasn't always possible. In one such case, a man came in with a unique double-headed coin that he believed was worth a fortune. "I had to delicately point out to him that it was in fact two coins glued together," McBride said.

His most memorable walk-in was a man who claimed to have come back from the dead.

"It started in very ordinary fashion," McBride said. "A call to the news desk from reception to say a man was there with a story. I obviously didn't duck quickly enough when Stuart [the news editor] took the call and I was sent out, notebook in hand. It was a well-established routine. Meet and greet, quickly establish credibility and if you thought it worthwhile take them into the interview room. This room, to the side of reception, was painted a revolting green colour, which must have come as a cheap job lot as I've since seen similar rooms in government buildings around the country."

"So on this particular day 'Mr Walkin' seemed very credible but the alarm bells should have started when he whispered that this was a very delicate, important subject that he couldn't discuss in reception. As we moved to the interview room, we chatted about the forthcoming rugby internationals and everything seemed OK until the moment he sat down and said: 'I was killed last week but I've come back to life and I want to let the *Echo* readers know how they can return from the afterlife'. That didn't just ring the alarm bells; by then they were screaming at me and a large red flag was waving in my face."

"Now the usual routine was that if you were sent to deal with a walk-in, and hadn't reappeared within a certain time or phoned upstairs to let them know you were OK, someone from the news desk would come to rescue you. But it could be at least twenty minutes. So I went through the mental checklist of who, why, what, when and how to fill the minutes. In fairness to 'Mr

Walkin' he was calm, measured and sounded perfectly plausible – apart from the fact he had come back from the dead."

"His story was that he had been shot and killed – he wouldn't say by whom or why – but the power of positive thought had revived him. I was too polite to question how his brain continued to function after being killed. He was most insistent that everybody could do the same mental process. They were the longest twenty minutes of my life and I've never been so grateful for anyone's knock at the door. Stuart bounded in, told me there was an urgent call upstairs for me and we jointly shepherded Mr Walkin from the room, through reception and out of the front door."

. . .

While Mr Walkin claimed to have come back from the dead, Eryl Crump met a man who stormed in and bellowed: "I'm alive!"

It was about 2010, and Crump was working on the North Wales edition of the *Daily Post*, based in the Caernarfon office which was shared with the weekly *Caernarfon and Denbigh Herald*.

"The newsroom was on the top floor, so it was a four-staircase walk to reception," he said. On this occasion, the receptionist called to say a visitor had an issue with that day's paper, so Crump walked downstairs.

"Standing in our cosy front office... was a clearly irate gentleman," he said. "Seeing me, he took a step towards the counter and slapped down a copy of the paper." The man roared, "I'm alive", then stormed out and went across the road to the local Wetherspoons. Crump added: "He returned from the pub a short time later, having calmed down a bit – and seemingly having handed back the paper he had 'borrowed' from the bar staff."

It turned out the man had the same name and age as a man who had been found dead in a river at the weekend. "His name now escapes me but it was an unusual name for North Wales and it was normal practice not to detail the full address in case of unwanted attention," Crump said. The visitor eventually saw the funny side of the story, having been mocked by his friends. Crump added: "It is a local joke that many people buy the paper to check the BMDs (births, marriages and deaths) in case they had died."

• • •

In the early 2000s, Richard Edwards (appeared in

Chapter Two, lost medal story) was asked to write about a man who wanted to make it clear that – contrary to local rumours – he was very much alive. Edwards worked at the *York Evening Press*, then based in an old-fashioned office with facilities including an outside toilet with a pull-chain.

"One day I was typing away in the room at the back and this bloke came in and I heard him talking to the receptionist," he said. As Edwards and his colleagues registered what the man was saying, they stopped to listen in amazement. "Word had somehow got around the town that he had died," he said. "Sympathy cards just started to arrive at this poor bloke's house even though he was alive."

The not-dead man lived in Norton, North Yorkshire – a tight-knit community where most people knew each other – and his efforts to kill the zombie story had backfired. "The more he rang people telling them he was alive, the more sympathy cards turned up," Edwards said. The paper ran a front-page story to clear up the confusion, under the headline: "I'm not dead."

"Hopefully we did a bit of good public service," Edwards said, adding: "The photo was of him posing with a load of cards."

Edwards admits his heart sank at being called to

deal with walk-ins, but he said: "I was often called to help at reception because I was generally pretty diplomatic and good at getting people out."

These diplomatic skills were tested one day when he saw a visitor sitting in reception – a man Edwards knew to be the "hardest man in York". Edwards approached, and recalls thinking: "I've really got to tread carefully here."

The man was known as Tote, but when Edwards asked his name, the man replied: "I am that I am." Taking cover behind an age-old journalistic shield – "can you spell that for me?" – the name became: Iyam Thatiam. Simultaneously terrified and struggling not to laugh, Edwards tried to get the interview over with.

"It was almost like he had decided to test me," he said. "I managed to keep my poker face and got whatever his story was out of him." Despite the meeting being etched in his memory, Edwards cannot recall what the story itself was about. "I wish I could remember it, but probably the reason is I was concentrating so hard on not getting on the wrong side of him."

Edwards "strained every sinew" to get the story in the paper, and to get the details right, because he didn't want Mr Thatiam coming back to complain. After a nervy fortnight, word reached Edwards that the man –

who had reverted to the name Tote for reasons that are lost to history – was happy with the article. Edwards would live to see another deadline day.

CHAPTER SIX

Reporters under fire: Hostage, handcuffs & 'fuck you too!'

REVIEWS OF MY JOURNALISTIC EFFORTS have not always been positive. The chairman of a local football club once waited patiently on hold so he could call me a "twat". Perhaps word got around that I was hard to reach by phone, because soon after that a visitor came in and screamed: "You'd better have deep fucking pockets because I'm taking you for every penny you've got." We never heard from him again.

Among the many charming people who walked into our little office in Dorking, a particular couple stand out in my memory. They had appeared several times before local magistrates. In October 2010, they admitted animal neglect after failing to provide food or basic medical care to their dogs. It made a page lead in our paper. Unsurprisingly, the pair were not delighted about this, so they popped in for a chat.

It started badly. Our article had included a mention

of the woman's mental health problems, which had been offered by their lawyer in mitigation. The husband invaded my personal space before telling me I had called his wife "a mental", which was the same as using a racial slur, and therefore I was a racist. Before waiting for my defence to this charge, he launched into a fifteen-minute lecture in which various imaginary legal precedents were used as threats. When I eventually got frustrated and said I had some legal training (NCTJ Media Law and a copy of McNae on my desk) he replied: "Yeah, you look like someone who knows about media law."

Looking back, such feedback seems funny (although I failed to act on it, so I probably still look like someone who knows about media law). But stories like this are a fragment of a bigger picture: journalism involves interfering in people's lives, often against their wishes. You weigh up the rights and wrongs, but you will inevitably annoy and upset some people. These may very well be scary people, and as a local reporter you rarely have the safety of a large press pack. I once waited alone outside Crawley Magistrates' Court to take a court snatch (a photo of a defendant outside court). When the man appeared and I took the picture, he called me a "fucking mug" and gave a highly detailed description of what he would do to me if his picture appeared in the paper. His plan was essentially an amateur autopsy, but back then I was recklessly keen on my job so – despite living in the same town as this alarming fellow – I cheerfully trotted back to the office and filed the photo.

On another court job, a defendant – a serving police officer accused of assaulting his wife – waited inside Hayward Heath Magistrates Court until the sun went down. Cameras are not permitted in court – hence the need to catch people arriving or leaving – and this was the winter, so he presumably (and correctly) thought my cheap camera would struggle if he waited for cover of darkness. When the national media cover high-profile cases, defendants have to shove their way through a crowd of reporters and cameras. In this case, I was alone in the dark, shivering and wondering if he had found a back exit. But then he came out, surrounded by a huddle of friends who had come to court to support him. These pals were police officers too, and they shuffled out like one half of a rugby scrum, shielding their friend from me.

So far, so fair. I was entitled to take a picture; they were entitled to march like a miniature Roman legion. But then one of them broke away and brought his face uncomfortably close to mine. He began with a faux-friendly speech along the lines of "come on, mate, do you really need to...". When I told him I was entitled to be here, and that he shouldn't stop me doing my job, the fake smile dropped off his face. I still remember his snarling expression as he backed me against a wall, keeping me there until his friend had been driven away. This upstanding officer gave me a charming "cheers mate" before leaving. He never touched me, but it was a masterclass in intimidation. I've been punched by a large, angry man in the street, yet this cop was far scarier.

What I needed in that situation was someone bold and brash, someone unwilling or incapable of being intimidated. In my experience, plenty of local news photographers fit this description, and one in particular got me out of trouble with a magnificent display of bluff and confidence. Take a bow, Kevin Shaw. It was the late noughties, and I had heard that the far-right British National Party (BNP) was holding a meeting near Crawley. Kevin and I went along and sidled into the back row, using body language and facial expressions to blend in to this race-obsessed crowd. Then two things happened at once. The BNP's controversial leader, Nick Griffin, appeared at the front. And two gigantic, tattooed security men appeared at the back, looming over Kevin and me.

"Who the fuck are you?" one of them enquired. As

I silently prepared to die, Kevin leapt up and – being about six foot six – conducted a sort of counter-loom by towering over the guards.

"Hello, gents," he began, apparently excited to meet them. "We're from the *Crawley News*. Where do you want us? Can I set up over there for the pictures?"

I assume they had intended to throw us out, but Kevin's assertiveness seemed to bypass this, forcing them to answer his questions about the best place to get good lighting. We had sneaked in undercover, but Kevin simply rewrote that little piece of history and forced everyone to accept his version of events. I don't know what would have happened if Kevin hadn't been there, but I doubt I would have got the double-page spread that actually resulted. Every reporter should have a Kevin Shaw with them at all times, but journalism is often a solitary profession – and sometimes a dangerous one.

• • •

"Biggest story ever, a few feet over my head, and I missed it."

So tweeted Rob Campbell, referring to an incident at the *North Herts Gazette* in the mid-1980s. Campbell was a trainee reporter at the time, working at an old-fashioned office whose large ground-floor windows looked out into Hitchin marketplace. About fifteen reporters, subs and editors worked in a back room on the ground floor, while advertising was upstairs – along with a small, windowless storeroom that was sometimes used for interviews.

On this particular day, reception phoned to say a man had arrived. One of Campbell's colleagues – also a trainee – went to see the visitor. Campbell said the newsroom was busy – "we were working away, with about fifteen typewriters tapping and phones ringing" – so no one paid much attention to the trainee leaving. But about an hour later, his absence became glaring when the police phoned to ask about the "hostage situation".

"We still didn't really know what was going on," Campbell said. "The police arrived, and we were aware that my fellow trainee reporter was trapped in the little interview room upstairs. Sometime later, [the trainee] appeared back in the office and the police led a guy away."

The freed hostage explained that his captor had walked in with a story about the police confiscating his moped. They went upstairs to talk, at which point the visitor said he had a knife. He wanted his moped back, and he made the reporter phone the police to demand its return – or else. In what might seem an underreaction by modern standards, two police officers arrived and spoke to the hostage taker through the keyhole of the interview room.

"Eventually he came out and they took him away," Campbell said. "What made us laugh at the time was that the first we knew about it was when the police called us."

. . .

Three decades later, in 2017, Thomas Haworth found himself in similarly hot water – but in his case it was the police themselves doing the hostage taking. Sort of. Called downstairs to reception in the large – and, by this time, half empty – office of the *Swindon Advertiser*, Haworth met a man in his seventies, speaking broken English in a strong Italian accent. The man wanted to place a notice in the paper about a 9/11 memorial he had organised.

However, because the event had already taken place, Haworth said a notice didn't really make sense – and instead offered a write-up. This apparently innocuous distinction outraged the man, who was "adamant" he would get his notice published. He finally left, deflected but not defeated.

"A couple of days later, reception called and said, 'he wants to speak to you'," said Haworth, who went downstairs to find the small man gesticulating angrily. "He was rather furious and he presented a picture of himself, in his thirties maybe, as an Italian policeman. He told me again that I needed to put [his notice] in the paper."

The man had more than just a photograph from his time with the Italian police. He still had his handcuffs, and he attempted to arrest Haworth. He grabbed the reporter's wrists, fighting to get the handcuffs on, but age had weakened his grip and Haworth successfully resisted arrest. The paper's receptionist – who had howled with laugher at the scene unfolding before her – now recovered and managed to usher the irate former lawman from the premises.

The photo of the policeman in his uniform was somehow left behind – perhaps as a warning against future journalistic crimes – and it stayed on Haworth's desk. Sadly, the picture is now lost, but the memory remains. Haworth said: "I still live in Swindon and I see him occasionally and think 'that's the guy who perhaps, in his own head, still thinks he's a policeman'."

• • •

In about 2010, an irate reader decided to bypass legal measures and dish out some corporal punishment to reporter Dara Bradley.

"She demanded that our receptionist, Kathleen, bring to her the journalist who had written an article in that day's *Galway City Tribune*, which she felt was disparaging to birds, and in particular, if I recall correctly, seagulls," Bradley said. "This slightly eccentric bird enthusiast – think Brenda Fricker in *Home Alone Two* – was not pleased with the argument I put forward in defence of the article, and she proceeded to attack me with her handbag. The aim of her swing was, thankfully, not very good and the leather bag did not make a connection – but her roaring and shouting at me certainly hit home. She was eventually persuaded by Kathleen, and a member of our advertising team, to leave the front office, and to write a letter of complaint to the editor."

• • •

This next story takes some telling. Cast your mind back – if it goes that far – to 1979, and the sex scandal surrounding MP and Liberal Party leader Jeremy

Thorpe. If you don't remember it, or need a refresher, there's a book and a BBC series (starring Hugh Grant) both called: *A Very English Scandal*. In short, to quote Wikipedia: "The scandal arose from allegations by Norman Josiffe (otherwise known as Norman Scott) that he and Thorpe had a homosexual relationship in the early 1960s, and that Thorpe had begun a badly planned conspiracy to murder Josiffe, who was threatening to expose their affair."

As Thorpe prepared to go on trial, Jon Smith was a young reporter who had recently joined the *Acton Gazette* in West London. Smith's connection to the story does not begin with a walk-in – but, as you'll see, it ends with one. Coming to London from the *Bedford County Times*, Smith lived in a shared house in Harrow. His landlord – who Smith described as "quite mad" – lived there too. Smith quickly learned to be sceptical about his landlord's claims, including a repeated assertion that he was a "big mate" of Andrew Newton – the man allegedly hired by Jeremy Thorpe to kill Norman Josiffe.

"I thought he was fantasising," Smith said. "I just took it with a pinch of salt." So he was stunned when Andrew Newton turned up at the house, and became a regular visitor. This was the period between Thorpe's initial court hearing and his trial, so journalists had been warned – on "pain of death", as Smith put it – not to speak to anyone involved in the case. However, the story had come right to his front room, with Newton returning night after night to talk about the case. The landlord knew Smith was a journalist, but Smith didn't know whether this had been explained to everyone present.

"I assumed that Andrew Newton did [know] but I didn't want to break the flow by... broaching the subject," he said. Newton spoke at length during his visits, drinking bottles of Dubonnet as he did so. After Newton left, Smith would return to his room and write down what he had heard. He had plenty of material for a fascinating story once the trial finished – but much of this became useless when Thorpe was found not guilty. This left Smith with a "story about a gunman who never was a gunman".

He was disappointed, and perhaps his news editor was too – because she sent him to door-knock "your mate Andrew Newton" to get his view of the verdict. A photographer was sent as well, leading to a bizarre misunderstanding.

"I got there and he [Newton] drove up in his car and told me to get in quick. He said, 'there's a photographer'. I didn't tell him it was our photographer." Stranger still, Newton appeared to be unaware of the news from the Old Bailey. "We put the radio on and heard the verdict on LBC," Smith said. The excitement over, Smith returned to the office and wrote his "much-sanitised" background piece about the case.

He soon moved out of the shared house, and – not seeing Newton for a couple of months – he moved on from the story. But the story wasn't finished with him. Sitting in the *Acton Gazette*'s "smoke-befuddled little office" one day, Smith got a call from reception saying Andrew Newton had arrived to place a classified advertisement to sell a car. The news editor told the receptionist to keep him talking, then turned to Smith and said: "Your mate Andrew Newton is downstairs. You ought to go and talk to him."

Smith replied: "No, I don't really think that's a good idea." Although he had kept his profession ambiguous previously, Smith felt sure Newton knew by now that he was a reporter – not least because his picture byline had appeared along with the backgrounder about the case. Things had gone "belly up" for Newton since the trial, Smith said, adding that he had a "fair idea what state of mind this guy might be in". Perhaps it was best to let this walk-in walk out.

Like all good news editors, Smith's superior carefully considered these valid points and decided that, on balance, Smith should do as he was told and go to see

Newton. Right now. "I had argued with the news editor for long enough for Andrew Newton to have gone out the door," Smith said.

Catching up with Newton outside the *Gazette*'s King Street office, Smith – with some reluctance – called out: "Andrew!" Things happened quickly. Newton looked at Smith and swore. Smith's next recollection is regaining consciousness on the pavement, realising he had been "felled" with one punch.

"He broke my glasses. I sort of struggled back in [to the office], probably with a bloody nose, looking like I had been dragged through a hedge backwards – or punched by a hitman." Showing a depth of sympathy known only to senior staff at newspapers – and perhaps the occasional executioner – his news editor declared this a "good story".

Smith didn't think so, fearing that Newton would come back and hit him again if the paper published the story. Given the complexity of the situation – including the details of how Smith had got so much information from Newton – the news editor finally conceded that it was best not to publish after all. Smith was relieved: "We decided to let Mr Newton have some privacy, and I could stay in one piece."

THERE'S SOMEONE IN RECEPTION

. . .

Also during Smith's time at the *Acton Gazette*, he was called to reception because "two blokes from the Sweeney" were down there. The receptionist informed him that the two police officers in question were "cross". Reluctantly going downstairs, Smith found the visitors looking through back-copies of the newspaper, which were kept on wooden spines in reception.

"I said, 'help yourself', but he [one of the officers] kept looking at me and said, 'come over here'. He said, 'what are you fucking playing at?'" When Smith expressed honest confusion at this, the officer added: "Do you want to call the fucking reporter off?"

It gradually emerged that a reporter had visited the house of a woman who was under police protection, because she was the wife of a "supergrass" providing evidence in a major investigation. However, these bloodhounds of the law were on the wrong scent – the reporter in question was from the *Acton Gazette*'s sister paper, the *Ealing Gazette*. Both known locally as *the Gazette*, this was understandable – but Smith said: "I obviously couldn't call them off because I hadn't put them on." He could have corrected the officers' misunderstanding, but he saw no reason to help them. He simply apologised and let them leave.

"They came back a few days later because the *Ealing Gazette* reporter had gone back and knocked on her door again," he said. The officers were angry and told Smith: "You are going to screw this whole thing up." The police said they had been forced to move the woman to a new location, at great cost.

The supergrass case was making headlines, and Smith spotted a possible scoop. One of the officers had now worked out his mistake regarding the two *Gazettes* – and found himself "in a bind because he had just spent taxpayers' money moving the woman". Knowing that the officer would not want this made public, Smith suggested sending a feature writer from his paper to meet the woman they were protecting – to write a piece (with no names or pictures) about life in hiding. The officer agreed – and became a good contact in Smith's remaining time in Acton.

"I never minded working with ambiguity like that," Smtih said. "He [the officer] has come banging into my office, swearing at me. My view was always that you don't need to play nicey nicey with these guys. If I could put one over on them, I would – and I did."

Smith accepts that his tales of local journalism in the 1970s might seem strange by modern standards. However, he went on to work for the *Sun*, and recalled a large placard on the wall that staff would see as they left the newsroom: "Do it to them before they do it to you."

• • •

Irene Kettle remembers the "dark days when it was rare for the editor to be female". It might sound like the 1970s or earlier, but this was 1997, and Kettle was the first female editor of the *Colchester Gazette*. One day she got a call from reception. The normal policy for walk-ins was to send the "newest, greenest reporter you can find", but this visitor specifically asked for the editor. This might have set alarm bells ringing, but the receptionist's tone gave no hint of problems.

"She obviously didn't think there was anything wrong," Kettle said. But when she arrived downstairs, things escalated quickly. The paper received a daily delivery of milk in glass bottles, and the receptionist hadn't spotted that the man – whose hands were behind his back – had picked up one of these. As Kettle appeared, he pulled the bottle out and smashed it on the receptionist's desk, shouting: "I'm going to fucking kill him." But there was no him to kill. The man's preconception about editors being male gave Kettle a way out.

"The idea that the editor was a woman didn't cross

his tiny little brain," said Kettle, who would normally have corrected such an error. "I decided on that one and only occasion that discretion was the better part of keeping myself out of hospital."

She told the man: "Really sorry. The editor isn't here. I'm just the secretary." Dropping his aggression in a flash, the man replied: "Okay, love, I'll come back another time." Then he left – and never came back, so Kettle never found out what his complaint was about.

This wasn't Kettle's only brush with imminent violence. As a reporter, she was covering Colchester Magistrates' Court when the news desk called to send her to an illegal rave. Still in her smart court attire, she went to the middle of nowhere with nothing but a notebook and a photographer for protection. She arrived to discover that the police were – perhaps wisely – keeping their distance from the crowd of revellers. Kettle and the photographer had to proceed, so they crossed a field full of people "off their heads" and a remarkably high population of pit bulls.

"These great big guys surrounded us and said, 'Give us the fucking camera'," Kettle said. With reckless bravery, the photographer refused – and Kettle remembers thinking: "Oh God, I'm going to die." Worse, the photographer then walked away, leaving her alone with the enraged rave-goers.

But he soon came back, and suggested that the men could take the film from the camera – but not the camera itself. They agreed to this, and a "gorilla of a guy" snatched the film. Only once they were safely away did the photographer tell Kettle that he had quickly swapped the film for a blank one while his back was turned. "Don't worry," he told her. "I've got the pictures."

• • •

As Kettle's story shows, surviving journalism isn't all about handling the public – you also have to put up with your colleagues. At the *Pontefract and Castleford Express*, Ellen Beardmore (appeared in Chapter One, stolen wallet story) thought she had fallen foul of a reader. It happened after the paper ran an Easter competition, with three large chocolate eggs as prizes. Two were claimed, but the third sat untouched in the office for several weeks.

Assuming the winner was not coming, the staff – including Beardmore – ate the egg. A few hours later, a man arrived to claim it. Beardmore answered the door, stalled the visitor and ran back into the newsroom in the vain hope of finding another chocolate egg to hand out. "Everyone was laughing their heads off," Beardmore said.

As it turned out, the joke was on her. One of her colleagues had met a friend outside and asked him to ring the doorbell and pretend he had won the Easter egg. Beardmore said she learned a valuable lesson: "It taught me to leave the prizes alone."

• • •

I also experienced the acid humour of a colleague when, at the *Crawley News* in the late 2000s, I was offered a glamorous press trip to New York. The borough of Crawley includes Gatwick Airport, and I assume that's how the offer came about – maybe an airline had launched a new regular flight to the Big Apple. Anyway, the proposed trip included a fancy meal, and my friendly (jealous) co-worker told me: "I hope you choke on your gala dinner."

I never went on the trip – or any stylish free holiday. I did once get a free ticket to Chessington World of Adventures, on the proviso that I write a review. Being an honest newshound, my write-up noted that the park did not live up to the standards I recalled from joyous childhood visits. Chessington responded by asking me not to visit again. So, no gala dinner, but I wasted my free go on the Vampire Ride.

• • •

Hannah Postles (appeared in Chapter Two, grenade story) looks back and laughs about a tale from the *Pontefract and Castleford Express*, though at the time it was far more troubling than any office politics. While working in the paper's Pontefract office, she was called to reception and found a woman clutching a black hoodie. Clearly uncomfortable, the woman said: "Are you Hannah Postles? I've got something here and I think I should give it to you." In white lettering on the hoodie were the words: "Sex for information. Contact Hannah Postles at the Pontefract and Castleford Express." A local police officer was named on the back.

"The lady was really apologetic," Postles said. "She worked in the charity shop across the road, and the staff had been going through rails of clothes and found the hoodie. They thought someone must have put it on the rail, because it hadn't gone through the shop's system and been given a price."

Postles continued: "I thought someone must have placed it there because the shop was so close to our office, so maybe they thought it would reach me. I remember going back upstairs and colleagues asking me 'what was that all about?' You don't know how to react to being given something like that. I didn't know whether to laugh or cry. I was just thinking 'why has somebody done this and what message are they trying to send me?' It took me quite a while to realise just how menacing it was."

"I had my suspicions about who had done it, which made me feel even more uncomfortable," Postles said. "I think it was connected to a court case I covered, because the police officer whose name was on the jumper had helped me with it." Postles said her colleagues – an all-female editorial team – were really supportive. "They made sure I wasn't in the office alone at any point, and we walked to our cars together after work."

Nothing more came of it, and Postles and her friends now jokingly refer to the hoodie as the "sex jumper". However, reflecting on the story, Postles said: "People don't always realise how vulnerable you can be as a reporter. A lot of work you do puts you in situations that aren't very safe. Colleagues don't always know where you are and who you're going to see."

* * *

Lee Marlow (appeared in Chapter Four, Paralympian story) also found himself in a worrying situation after reporting on a court case. He worked at the *Leicester*

Mercury, a paper he had delivered as a boy. Recalling the day in 1996 when he got the job as a reporter, he said: "I don't think there was a prouder man in the East Midlands." Having such strong local links comes with pros and cons. "I was reporting in the town where I went to school and where I went out at the weekend," he said.

The court case in question involved a local "bad lad" who had been arrested for car theft so often that the police nicknamed him "Wheels". Marlow remembered Wheels from school – and Wheels remembered Marlow. Turning around in court, Wheels had said: "Just fucking make me sound alright."

Marlow reported the court case – which in his view made Wheels look bad – and that Friday night they saw each other in a local nightclub. Wheels approached, and Marlow expected some rough words at the very least. But Wheels said: "Marlow! Read your report. Like it. Good job."

Not every experience of Marlow's career went as smoothly as his nightclub brush with Wheels. He was "threatened by man who lived on my street who buried his dad in his back garden," and also recalled being chased in the line of duty. This might have sent some people running for a new career, but Marlow concluded: "All fairly standard stuff for a local hack, really."

* * *

Crouching in a cupboard, knees burning from holding this position for thirty minutes and counting, Tony Earnshaw doubted his career choice. Outside the cupboard were his desk, his office, his colleagues. So, why hide here? The answer was out there too, prowling among the desks, lecturing anyone who would listen. It was spring 1988, and Earnshaw was a trainee reporter at the *Spenborough Guardian* in West Yorkshire. The man beyond the cupboard door was a reader of the paper, and a prolific writer of letters to the editor. A man with *views*.

"The office was in an old Victorian building in Cleckheaton, and all the reporters were shoved together in this one room," said Earnshaw, who had joined the paper a few months earlier, aged twenty-one. Visitors came in via a small reception downstairs, and the journalists could hear people coming before they appeared. Earnshaw said this particular visitor was "bombastic" – a "notorious racist", a "quasi-Enoch Powell" whose letters bristled with hateful ideology. The other reporters had seen him many times, but Earnshaw – "fresh-faced with my new suit" – gave him a fresh audience. When they first met, the man had barked "who are you, then?" before launching into a long speech.

"I became aware that most reporters in the room were desperately focussing on what they were doing," Earnshaw said. "They didn't want to engage with this guy. He was awful." During several visits in Earnshaw's early months in the job, the man always cornered him for a fresh lecture. Earnshaw was "perhaps too polite" to discourage him. But one day, on hearing the detested booming voice, followed by feet thumping up the stairs, Earnshaw recalls thinking: "Oh fuck this."

"I got out of my chair, and behind me was a low cupboard," he said. "I climbed inside it and shut the door." Two other reporters were in the office at the time and, as both were adept at ignoring this visitor, Earnshaw supposed the visit would be brief.

"He talked for forty minutes," Earnshaw said. "There was no opportunity for me to climb out, so I had to stay there squatting. I was terrified of moving, in case I made a noise or nudged the door open." Eventually, the man left. "I kind of tumbled out. My legs were on fire," said Earnshaw. He had successfully avoided the dreaded visitor, but his pride and thigh muscles couldn't support this approach for long. "After that, whenever he came in, I had to just sit at my desk and suffer it," he said.

• • •

Mandy Langley (appeared in Chapter One, lock-switch story) dodged a decidedly unhappy customer at the *South Wales Argus* in spring 1990. The visitor, a weightlifter, had recently been stripped of a medal after failing a drugs test. He had also appeared in court for shoplifting, and Langley reported on the case.

"After my story appeared in the paper, this gold-medal-standard, anabolic-steroid-using weightlifter turned up in reception to complain, with a brace of pit-bull-like dogs on chains," Langley said. "Thankfully, I was out." And, happily for Langley and her colleagues, he didn't call in again.

• • •

Happily for me, I was on holiday when an outraged reader visited the *Crawley News* in 2008.

"It was a normal boring morning in our little newsroom, which was up a flight of stairs from a doorway on our town's high street," said Michael Connellan, who was on duty that day. "Someone out on the street buzzed our door buzzer, saying that they wanted to speak to us about a story we'd run. So I pressed a button to let them in."

Connellan then heard feet stomping up the stairs. A moment later, a man burst into the newsroom and shouted: "Who's the editor around here?" Connellan indicated Glenn Ebrey, and the man approached and began slapping the desk.

"I realised we might have a bit of a problem," Connellan said. The visitor brandished a copy of our latest edition, open at the births, marriages and deaths page, and started screaming: "Who did this?" Ebrey suggested a calmer tone might be more constructive, upon which the man switched to kicking the desk.

"Seeing as I'd put our editor in the firing line, I decided I'd better help out," said Connellan, who joined colleagues in asking the man to leave. It didn't work, so he tried a tougher approach. "I picked up a skateboard that had been living under my desk after a photo story about the town's new skate park. Holding it by the axles, it felt like an effective shield and weapon at the same time. The screaming invader, not wanting a mouth full of skateboard, started backing down the stairs. Once he was outside, we locked the door."

But the man wasn't finished. He started kicking the door and succeeded in breaking the glass. Before he managed a second ascent of the stairs, the police arrived and arrested him. In the excitement, the team remained unclear on exactly what the man disliked so much in the paper. That got cleared up during a phone call the next day.

Ebrey answered and a quiet voice said: "I'm the idiot who stormed your office yesterday." The man explained that he had got his lover pregnant and – keen to conceal this from his wife – he had refused to acknowledge the child as his own.

Connellan continued: "As revenge, following the birth, the mother had submitted a photo of the bonnie baby to our births, marriages and deaths page, with a caption stating the name of the baby, the mother – and the father too. We'd printed it, assuming they were a happy couple, and unwittingly exposed him as a love rat to his wife as she read the paper over her cornflakes. Whoops."

. . .

Not all complaints come in the form of angry men at the door. Sometimes a gentle rebuke or even polite bafflement can cut journalists just as deeply. In the early 1990s, the *Stoke Sentinel* ran a straightforward story about an award won by a local Scout troop, along with a picture. At this time photographers provided hard copies of their images, along with hand-written captions. In this case, the writing was not the neatest –

and somehow one of the children appeared in the paper with the name "Ardsfur".

"Whoever subbed it didn't question it," said Nigel Wiskar (appeared in Chapter Three, duck potatoes story), who worked for the *Sentinel* at the time. The paper received a letter from the child's grandparents, saying how excited they were to see their grandson in the paper – and noting their disappointment about the caption. Not unreasonably, the grandparents pointed out that Ardsfur was not even a name.

"I showed this to a friend of mine who was thinking about being a journalist," Wiskar said, laughing. The friend became a journalist, partly inspired by the tale of Ardsfur – which presumably convinced him that journalism would be a laugh, if nothing else. In Wiskar's phone contacts, that friend is listed as Ardsfur.

Wiskar also worked at the *Manchester Evening News*, where he recalls a letter sent in by the people running a local cricket league. The note informed the paper – in painfully polite terms – that the match reports they had been publishing for some time were being written by a man who was not, in fact, attending the games. He was simply making them up. The league asked: "Can you please stop using these match reports?"

• • •

Similarly agonising politeness reached me in the post, while I was news editor of the *Dorking and Leatherhead Advertiser*. Here's the letter in full:

> *Sir, I saw the enclosed news item in the* Advertiser *two weeks ago. I am very intrigued to see that Leigh railway station has been fitted with CCTV. I have lived in Leigh for fifty-six years, but have never seen a railway station!! Please tell me where it is, as we are very short of bus services too! Very puzzled. Yours* [name redacted because, despite being seared into my memory, I don't have the guts to contact this correspondent to ask if I can use her letter. Imagine her puzzlement if I did].

I have absolutely no idea how the above error came about. Naturally, I blame everyone except myself. The note in my diary from the time simply says: "Sometimes in life, you just fuck up."

Other times, you don't do much wrong and you still find yourself in trouble. In 2011, a woman called our office in Dorking and asked us to publish a story about her aunt reaching the age of a hundred. Oddly, the caller refused to give her name, or tell us where her aunt lived – a pretty basic detail required for a local news story. When I refused to run it on this basis, the caller told me: "You are disgusting. I'm disgusted. You have ruined the poor lady's hundredth birthday."

I was also told "you've really ruined it for these boys" after we printed a story about some army cadets, along with a picture in which some of them were in the background, and therefore not as visible as their pals. The complainer said: "I only hope you can make up for it in a small way by publishing a double-page apology next week." OK. Two questions, though: how would a double-page apology in the local paper cheer the lads up, and how the hell would I fill those pages?

· · ·

Whether journalists choose to defend themselves or simply own up to an error, most conversations with unhappy readers involve a lot of listening and not much else. Whether you've made a mistake or not, the complainer usually wants to have their say – and in many cases that's the end of it. But sometimes, just sometimes, journalists bite back.

One such example involved Polly Rippon (appeared in Chapter One, "legless killer" story) at the

Sheffield Star. Rippon had covered a court story that led to a series of aggrieved calls and visits. A local cross-dresser had been convicted of assault, and was – to put it mildly – dissatisfied with the *Star*'s coverage.

"He said he was going to get our website shut down," Rippon said. Showing the opportunism of all good reporters, Rippon requested an interview and wrote a story. But this didn't satisfy the complainer, who phoned after the interview was published, demanding to speak to someone more senior. Rippon only heard her deputy editor's side of the ensuing call, which ended – in a moment that has passed into newsroom folklore – with the words: "And fuck you too!"

During our conversation, Rippon highlighted the immense value of local newspaper receptionists, who provided the first line of defence against troublesome walk-ins. "The sad thing is that we used to have a reception staffed by three women who had worked at the paper for a long time," she said. "They were so used to dealing with people who came in." When reporters arrived to meet a walk-in, a receptionist would often "give you a bit of a look", Rippon said – conveying their experienced opinion on whether this would result in a story or simply waste everyone's time.

An unhappy reader talked herself into trouble at the *Caernarfon & Denbigh Herald* in the late 1990s. Eryl Crump (appeared in Chapter Five, "I'm alive" story) used to attend the local magistrates' court on Mondays, picking up stories for publication each Thursday. This time, a drunk driver had appeared in court after failing to stop for police. She claimed she had feared being assaulted by fake police officers, but had been advised by her solicitor to plead guilty. The magistrates fined her and banned her from driving.

"At that stage the story was filler and was allocated a space on page sixteen," Crump said. "But she visited the office and insisted on speaking to the reporter [who had been] in court. That would be me. She said I had not asked her permission to be in court for her case, to which I explained the normal procedure, and she left." Annoyed by her attitude, the team decided to bump the story up to a page lead. And it wasn't over yet.

"She returned later with a gentleman friend and asked for my superior," Crump said. "We nearly sent Ben the trainee but the news editor went and heard the same tale. The story moved up the news list to page seven. It moved up again when she harangued the editor on the phone, and would have been that week's splash had she called in again."

* * *

Martin Robinson went to even greater lengths after a schoolteacher tried to get one over on the *Otley and Ilkley Times*. The paper received a letter from someone suggesting the setting up of a "whistling revival society".

"It went something on the lines that in days gone by the delivery boy or postman would go about his work with a cheery whistle, but now would most likely have a set of headphones instead," Robinson explained. "I immediately thought 'what a nice story' and set off to find the author of the letter for further details." But the house number from the letter didn't exist.

"I tried the nearest one to it," said Robinson. "A woman answered the door and, when I explained what I was after, looked shifty and said she knew nothing about it. When I said to her that I suspected she did know about the letter, she confessed that her partner, a teacher at a local comprehensive, had sent it as a school exercise to see just what trivia newspapers would publish, especially in summer."

Thanking the woman, Robinson left. An idea was forming, and back at the office he wrote it up as a front-page story – calling for the revival of the noble art of whistling.

"It was picked up by TV and several nationals," said Robinson. "Soldiers were whistling on parade at Aldershot [army base]." The story also led to the creation of a whistling contest in the town's civic hall.

And what of the teacher? He was "whistled at everywhere he went in Otley," Robinson said, adding: "It served him right and I can't say I had any sympathy for him." Don't mess with the local press.

CHAPTER SEVEN
The ones that count

DESPITE THE MANY MEMORABLE STORIES provided by journalists for this book, there's no denying that many – let's be honest, most – walk-ins amount to little or nothing. You listen, and maybe give some directions or politely suggest the visitor tries the rival newspaper. Sometimes you get a nib, a picture story or a letter to the editor (all useful of course). But reporters could be forgiven for thinking walk-ins are a waste of time.

Mark Hanna might have fallen into this trap when a self-confessed drug addict (who I'll call Eric) walked into the office of the *Sheffield Star* in 1988. Eric's story was barely believable, and his addiction alone might have put some reporters off. But Hanna and his colleague Jeremy Watson listened – and what they heard chimed with a previous tip-off and existing concerns about a local doctor.

Eric told them the doctor was selling drugs to addicts. In words overused on social media: huge if true.

But a hard story to tell. Hard even to investigate. How do you make the slightest enquiries without being crushed by a massive cartoon anvil marked "legal action"? With great care – and legal advice – Hanna and Watson edged onwards.

Eric was not a patient of the doctor in question, but he had a close friend who was. This friend, another addict, was referred to as Keith (not his real name) in the *Star*'s reports. Keith had already obtained drugs from the doctor. So, backed by their editor, the reporters gave Keith a tape recorder – and money to buy drugs. I asked Hanna how he came to trust Keith.

"Despite being a registered heroin addict, he was clever, calm and reliable in terms of turning up to meetings before the undercover operation began," Hanna said. "He was consistent in what he said, and did not try to explain things he had no knowledge of – these things are always good signs as regards whether someone is telling the truth. He gave us several, detailed witness statements. He grew to understand how much evidence we needed and that all detail had to be absolutely correct. Also, we made sure early on we knew where Keith lived and where his parents lived, so we could always be sure of contacting him."

Keith gave Watson, the health reporter, and Hanna permission to see his addiction records. So they trusted him to an extent, but Hanna added: "As regards the outcome of the investigation, we didn't need to trust him because the tapes and drugs, which we took from him immediately after he left the surgery after each visit, corroborated the allegations."

The end result? As Hanna put it: "Bingo." The *Star*'s front-page headline read: "City doctor sells drugs to addicts". The story described how the GP sold Keith an opium-based painkiller and an anti-nausea drug five times in fifteen days. Sheffield's doctors had been warned not to prescribe these two drugs together, as addicts were dissolving them and injecting the mixture. Several months before Hanna's investigation, the local pharmaceutical committee had written to this GP to ask him to stop prescribing this pairing, following complaints from local pharmacists.

The GP had followed this advice and stopped issuing these prescriptions – but, as the *Star* discovered, he began selling the drugs to addicts, who paid him as "private patients". He charged £5 for two tablets and even haggled for a higher price, the story revealed. When challenged by the paper, the doctor called this a consultation fee.

Despite the story, the doctor was neither struck off nor prosecuted. Hanna said the opioid drug was not a controlled one then, and so police "did not consider what he had done was criminal, but they were happy we had stopped him selling it to addicts".

. . .

One cold, wet Friday night in November 2019, a homeless man approached a brightly lit building. Having lost his home a year earlier, he had lived in temporary accommodation, then in a tent. Struggling with heroin addiction, even his camping gear was now gone. For the last six weeks, he had been sleeping rough – most recently in a graveyard. On entering the building – home of *BBC Three Counties Radio* in Dunstable – his message to the staff was simple: "Help me. I'm going to die."

This is perhaps the hardest kind of walk-in to deal with. The staff might have sent him on his way – sorry for the man, but feeling powerless to help. But Justin Dealey, a presenter and reporter, felt he had to do something. When somebody turns up like that, Dealey told me, they are absolutely desperate and a newspaper or radio station is "the last port of call".

"I will always listen to what they have to say," he said. "We're not social workers, but if there's something we can do to help, we will do." He added: "Part of me would have struggled to have slept that night if I had sent somebody back on the streets to sleep in a cemetery."

Dealey, who had reported extensively on homelessness and had slept rough in Milton Keynes to investigate and highlight the issues, said the man won his trust by being open about his addiction. On this particular Friday night, Dealey wasn't meant to be at work. He was only there to prepare for his show the next night, but he stayed late to record an "as-live" interview with the man for the next day's show. Producer Chris Milligan also stayed, and helped to find the man accommodation for that night, and a taxi to get him there. "We made some phone calls to get him some longer-term help," Dealey added.

A week later, they interviewed the man again, and he told them he had managed to secure a month-long stay in a hostel. "I've got the heating on – nice and warm by this radiator," he told them, adding that he was working hard to beat his addiction.

Three months later, Dealey was in Luton when someone shouted his name. At first, he didn't recognise the man who had called out – then he realised who it was. Speaking on his radio show, Dealey said: "I just could not believe what I was seeing, because the man that knocked on our door that night looked so ill. The man that I was looking at… looked so, so well. It was like a completely different person." The man agreed to be interviewed again, and invited Dealey to the shared house where he was now living.

"He was completely clean," Dealey told me, adding that the man had been allowed to see his son on his fifth birthday. "He had proved to social services that he wasn't taking drugs anymore." *BBC Three Counties Radio* had also earned a loyal listener. The man told them: "I listen to it every day."

Dealey accepted that many journalists might have been anxious about inviting a self-confessed drug addict into the studio, but he said: "I just thought 'you know what, if something [bad] does happen, I will take the blame for it'." He added: "The reason I've done alright in my career is because I've got a bit of heart – and you can't train that in somebody." And he said the role he and his colleague played was fairly easy: "All we had to do was get him in touch with the right people." The hard bit – dealing with the drug addiction – was for the man himself.

Dealey said he was determined to follow up the story – "good or bad". The result made a heart-warming interview, but Dealey doesn't know how the man's life has gone since then. He said: "In our job, you've got to do what you've got to do, then you've got to let people get on with their lives."

For some people with traumatic events in their past, telling their story can be a vital step towards moving on with their life. This was the case for a young man who visited the *Coventry Evening Telegraph* in 1992.

"This guy turns up in our office, asking to see a reporter," said Neil Benson, then the editor. He sent a reporter down, and half an hour later she came back with a shocking story. The visitor, a drug addict, claimed he had been sexually abused by a priest as a child. The priest in question was a larger-than-life character, one of the best-known people in the city.

"We thought long and hard about whether to run the story," Benson said. As we've seen, deciding whether to trust a source is one of the hardest parts of journalism. Benson's approach was to start by checking anything that could be checked. The walk-in gave various details. For example, he said he had been an altar boy in a particular church, and had gone on an under-elevens football trip to Ireland overseen by the priest. These details checked out, so the *Telegraph* team decided to proceed, albeit cautiously. They ran a story, naming no names, as what Benson called "a bit of a fishing expedition" to see if more victims came forward.

The reaction came in two forms: Benson was inundated with complaints, with many people phoning to shout about these outrageous accusations against a priest. "It was one of the first cases in the world where Catholic priests were being accused of abuse," he said. But there were other calls. By 6pm on the day of publication, six more victims had come forward – all naming the same priest as their abuser.

When approached for comments, the police were "tight lipped" and the church said nothing. Then it emerged that the priest had disappeared from Coventry and gone into a hospital known for treating people with alcoholism in his native Ireland. Not willing to let the story drop, Benson sent a reporter to Ireland. Asking questions at a pub near the hospital, the reporter was threatened with violence, and Benson agreed it was best to abandon this approach.

The priest later went to Australia, where he lived under a false name and reportedly died. News of his death was met with some scepticism, which only deepened when his family sent photographs to another UK newspaper, showing him lying in a coffin. "It was the first time they had seen a corpse laughing," said Benson, who tells the story in his memoir, *You Can't Libel the Dead*. Whether the priest's death was initially faked is unclear, but Australian authorities later confirmed he was indeed dead.

• • •

With drastic staff cuts and the shift of focus from print to online journalism in recent years, many people interviewed for this book said reporters today might struggle to find time to deal with walk-ins, which are often complex, messy tales that require lots of thought and effort.

Charles Thomson counts himself lucky that, in 2015, the *Yellow Advertiser* in Essex was "probably one of the last weekly newspapers in the country that actually functioned as a weekly newspaper in the sense that we didn't really have a functioning website". The paper was then part of the Tindle Group, whose owner remained focussed on print. "We did have a website," Thomson said. "But it was so useless that if you tried to upload a story to it, sometimes it would go offline for up to five hours."

While local competitors raced to be first with the news, Thomson said the *Yellow Advertiser* aimed to be "proactive rather than reactive", covering stories more deeply and doing longer-term investigative work. So, when he got a call from reception to say a man had come in with a story, Thomson had time to listen. The visitor had asked for him specifically – or rather, he asked to speak to the reporter who had written recent stories about out-of-court payments made by Essex County Council over allegations of historic child abuse.

Thomson had written two front-page stories a few months earlier, but his investigation had hit a dead end. He went downstairs – wondering if a new avenue was about to open – and met a white-haired man in a fedora, who introduced himself as Robin Jamieson. A retired NHS manager, Jamieson was rational, calm and measured. He told Thomson about a network of paedophiles that had existed in Southend in the late 1980s. He spoke of failures by the police and social services to investigate, and said only two suspects had been convicted – and they received prison sentences of just three and four years.

"The story he was telling was clearly very serious, and there was no feeling that he was over-egging it or exaggerating," Thomson said. With the crimes of Jimmy Savile making headlines at the time, Thomson said it "made sense that people would be coming forward" with stories of historic abuse.

Six months and lots of hard work went by before a story – the first of many – could be published. This led to more whistleblowers coming forward, and began a series of events that led to three further police investigations. Over a period of years, Thomson has won legal victories over access the criminal records of deceased people under the Freedom of Information Act. The investigation has also won multiple journalism awards, and was shortlisted for a Paul Foot Award.

Thomson admits some information may never be uncovered. Many of the men involved in the paedophile ring were known to their young victims only by first names or assumed names, and Thomson has searched – largely without success – for records of the people who owned the addresses used. But the depth and detail of his research – made possible by a walk-in – is remarkable. He tells the tale in a podcast series called "Unfinished: Shoebury's Lost Boys".

And he continues to investigate, showing the kind of determination that turned a walk-in into a complex investigation – a butterfly effect, as Thomson put it – with impacts far beyond the pages of a local paper.

• • •

Carl Eve investigated a strikingly similar criminal network for the *Plymouth Herald*. In 2013, while working in the iconic glass newspaper building called the Ship, Eve got a call from reception. A man wanted to speak about William Goad, a notorious paedophile who had been jailed for life nine years earlier. Although this court case happened before Eve joined the *Herald*, he was aware of claims that Goad was part of a wider network, most of whose members had never been prosecuted.

Working as a crime reporter, Eve had heard countless claims of bungled police investigations – and he had learned to treat them with a pinch of salt. But he quickly realised this was different. Arriving at reception, he met two people he recognised. He had seen them in court, at the trial of a paedophile linked to Goad. The man was a victim in the case. The woman was one of the investigating police officers.

They started talking. The man – who had repeatedly contacted the police and journalists about the wider network of abusers around Goad – explained that he had persuaded the police officer to come forward. The officer, who had retired due to long-term illness, said she had finally agreed that she needed to speak about failings in the investigation. She had reached the point where something needed to be done – and having made that decision she was utterly determined to expose the truth.

The officer said that, at the time of the original investigation, she had repeatedly voiced concerns to senior officers that other paedophiles linked to Goad were still at large. However, she said she heard an investigator being told to "put a lid on it and concentrate on Goad".

Eve said corroboration from the officer – "the woman at the heart of the investigation" – made his reporting possible. But he regretted the fact the victim had been ignored up to that point – including by journalists. "He was seen as a damaged man. Nobody took him seriously," Eve said, adding that many of Goad's victims had issues with alcohol, drugs and crime – and as a result "nobody sat down to listen".

"They are only seen as damaged people and yet everything they are saying is true once it's properly looked at and examined," he said. Another officer involved in the case later told Eve that many of the victims who came forward were known to him already – he had "rolled in the gutter" while trying to arrest them for various crimes. Now, knowing their history of abuse, the officer saw them differently. Speaking to them about their experiences, he understood that many were "nice but damaged people".

But doubt and disbelief were not restricted to the victims. Eve said the officer who walked into the *Herald*'s office "wasn't liked by the force" and her claims were met with "a lot of minimising" – suggestions that she might be exaggerating or lying. He said she was brave to come forward, and having done so she never wavered. She invited Eve to her house to look through boxes of paperwork related to the investigation.

"Every page was a story," he said. The only problem was the sheer volume. As Eve put it: "I've got absolute gold here, but there's a mountain." He needed at least a day to go through it all, but the news desk kept calling to hurry him up. Other stories needed finishing. In the end, he took photos of many of the documents. But even with the information now on his phone, Eve said he had "so much material and very little time to do it. I ended up doing it in the evening after I had put my kids to bed."

He got there in the end. A front-page story called for action to locate Goad's fellow abusers. The headline simply said: "Find them". It continued on four pages inside the paper, with further stories in the following days. Eve's reporting revealed that documents dating back as far as 1996 showed police were aware of allegations that Goad was part of a paedophile ring including "prominent men in society", and that boys were threatened to keep them quiet.

The reports sparked a flurry of action. The police launched a new investigation, and sources told the

Herald this had the potential to dwarf the inquiry into the crimes of Jimmy Savile. Goad had abused boys over a period of forty years. Sadly, with many of the perpetrators now dead, the investigation did not result in new criminal charges. Nothing could undo that damage done by the abusers. However, Eve's reporting at least gave a voice to the victims. They were, at last, taken seriously.

• • •

The significance of walk-in stories is not just the stories themselves. Many reporters interviewed for this book recalled certain walk-ins as important moments in their own lives. As a twenty-three-year-old trainee reporter, Shaun Jepson experienced a walk-in that taught him an important life lesson. Almost two decades on, Jepson said he still thinks about the man who wandered into reception at the *Derby Telegraph* that day.

"He reeked of booze, looked like he hadn't had a change of clothes in days," Jepson said. The man was red-eyed, and was so upset that he struggled to speak.

"[He] started to tell me the story of how his young son had died in his partner's arms and how they were both being fobbed off by the authorities when seeking answers," Jepson said. "I took notes. But my pre-judgement of this man, based on how he had presented himself, left me feeling it would probably amount to nothing, and that there would be an inevitable explanation."

"But I did pursue it. And over the course of many months, it transpired that this man and his family, and especially his son, had been tragically failed by the system, [the boy] dying from undiagnosed diabetes that a coroner ruled should have been caught had healthcare professionals spotted the clear warning signs that were there each time the family had sought medical attention prior to his death."

The man was about the same age as Jepson. Over time, as Jepson got to know the man, his partner and their other young child, he saw two parents who "absolutely worshipped their children and gave them all the love any child could wish for". They stayed in touch for some time, but Jepson moved on a few years later and subsequently fell out of contact.

"The whole experience though has stayed with me over all these years, and I suspect will do for the rest of my life," Jepson said. "I wish we had met in less tragic circumstances, but I was lucky to have met that man that day, because it changed me as a person forever. These stories are exactly why local journalism matters, and why it is the best and most rewarding job I'll ever do." He added: "It taught me at a young age never to judge someone by their appearance. You never know what someone is going through. It also taught me to be patient with people and listen closely to what they have to say."

• • •

Every journalist can relate to Jepson's experience of a story that sticks in the memory, and perhaps even changes the way we see the world. Deirdre O'Shaughnessy experienced this while working at the *Cork Independent* in 2011. The paper was fairly new and was based on an industrial estate, so walk-ins were rare. However, one day a woman walked in to place a classified advert. After taking details of the ad, a salesperson suggested the woman should speak to a reporter. O'Shaughnessy spoke to the woman, who explained that her granddaughter had so far survived despite being born with a rare condition that caused a malformed skull.

The grandmother had come to place a prayer of thanks in the paper. The child, then thirteen months old, had been expected to die before birth or soon after. But, with several surgeries already done and more to come, she had survived – a miracle, as her family saw it.

"They were just thankful," O'Shaughnessy said. "They were so proud of her." She kept in touch with the family for some time afterwards, and the girl continued to survive against the odds.

In a blog post, O'Shaughnessy wrote: "The times we are in encourage negativity and hopelessness, and it's difficult not to get sucked into the mire. A relentless barrage of bad news is enough to get most people down, and compounded by financial problems and uncertainty about jobs, bills and our futures, the gloom can be palpable at times." But she said the story of this child "shows that there is hope", adding: "Her very existence proves that life is a struggle, but it's worth fighting for. It proves that we can, sometimes, prevent the inevitable. It proves that it's always worth hoping, no matter what you are told."

CHAPTER EIGHT

Ring-ins & letters: Siege negotiator, stolen scarecrow & battle-tank surprise

IN MY FIRST WEEK AT THE *Crawley News* in August 2007, the phone rang and I picked it up. Nervous as I was, this felt like a major achievement. A lot seemed to rest on my new job, despite the terrible pay – which was barely enough to cover renting a room in a shared house containing a guy with a gambling problem who once threw a wardrobe down our stairs at night after losing a big bet. I had left university with a degree in history and politics, and had spent the three years since then working in pubs, travelling and trying (failing) to become a schoolteacher.

To this day, I believe that phone call changed everything. As you can tell by now, I love journalism (and, I hope, made a largely decent job of it). But I had expected to love teaching, and at some point in the training process I realised I hated it. I was terrified of hating journalism, of finding I couldn't do it, just as I had in the first hours standing in front of a school class.

The lady on the phone talked quickly and, having spent recent months sharpening my shorthand, I wrote down what she said. Even as a total rookie, I quickly realised this was *a story* – something worth putting in the paper. I think I even waved at the editor, as if to say: "Hold the front page". It wasn't deadline day. When the woman had told her tale, I asked questions. Lots of questions. I had something to cling to, and I wasn't letting go. I asked to come and see her, bringing a photographer, and to my surprise she agreed. Surely journalism couldn't be this easy.

The woman in question was a local mum of three (classic local news fact) who had bought a small gold charm – a piece of jewellery that attaches to a bracelet – on eBay for £14.91. The charm was damaged when it arrived, so she contacted the seller, who simply told her: "No refunds". Unwilling to accept that, she sent the charm back, got proof of posting and reported the situation to eBay and PayPal. Aside from a delightful email in which the seller threatened to break all the windows in her house, that was the last she heard of the situation for several months.

The police then visited her twice. The first time, they asked her to send the charm back to the seller, which she already had. Here's how she described the second visit: "One of them went to my bedroom and started going through my things, looking for a charm the size of a peanut. They searched for twenty minutes then told me I was going to be arrested even though they didn't find anything. They started leading me to the police car and I was angry so I said they should go the whole way and handcuff me. They agreed to this then put me in the back of the car."

It made our front page, under the headline: "Charming!" The picture, taken by her family, showed the woman being driven away by the police. She was wearing her pyjamas at the time, and she spent three hours in a cell and had a DNA sample taken before being released. As far as I can remember, no further action was taken against her.

It should be noted that this first exclusive of my career came at a cost. It's fair to say that the local police were not amused. I received a very long email from the sergeant whose job it was to deal with the press (or, as one of my two police-officer brothers says, "journo scum"). The sergeant took issue with... well, every single word I had written, plus the headline (this was written by a sub-editor, as is usually the case in newspapers). Some points were fair enough. For example, she made the reasonable argument that it's difficult for the police to weigh up such disputes about online purchases. Other points were harder to accept. For example, that I was an extremely bad journalist (jury still out at that stage) and human being (I plead not guilty). Despite this negative review, my journalism career had properly begun. I remain extremely glad I picked up that call.

Journalists dream of unearthing hidden stories, but the often-unpopular work of answering the phone or opening emails and letters can be just as valuable. With most local newspaper offices closed, reporters must do the simple – but easily overlooked – task of ensuring people can contact them. Phone numbers and email addresses should be listed and easy to find, unless there's a genuine safety reason to conceal them (for example when an individual journalist becomes the target of sustained abusive and/or threatening messages). At its most basic level, journalism is about talking to the public. Even cash-strapped local papers can afford a phone. When it rings, someone should answer it.

• • •

In November 2004, junior reporter Alex Lloyd answered the phone at the *York Evening Press*. It was lunchtime, shortly before the deadline for the final of the paper's four daily editions. It had been a normal shift, except that the staff "knew something was going on" in Heslington – a leafy suburb home to the University of York. Heslington was Lloyd's patch, and she had called the police press office to find out what was happening. They had not responded yet, but this caller was from Heslington. Lloyd expected it to be a member of the public with information about the incident.

The man on the line said: "I'm sat in my house and I've got about nine police officers pointing guns at me. They're telling me to come out and give up my gun." Stunned, Lloyd signalled to her news editor and tried to scribble a note to explain she was speaking to a gunman mid-siege.

"He was quite rambling and a bit confused," said Lloyd. "It was quite surreal. He was saying 'what should I do?' I told him 'I think you should probably go out and see the police'." The man replied: "But all my neighbours are going to see me." He was keen to avoid embarrassment, and stressed his gun was a replica.

"He felt he was in the right because it wasn't a real gun," Lloyd explained. Describing the pressure of being an accidental siege negotiator, she added: "I was trying to give sensible advice but not say the wrong thing."

The police then contacted the paper, asking Lloyd to hang up so they could speak to the man. Advising him to speak to the police immediately, she ended the call, which had lasted about fifteen minutes. Relieved, she rushed to write her copy, and her colleagues managed to find a picture of the man from a previous story in the paper's archive.

Meanwhile, the man gave himself up, and was later released on bail. In a detail that would catch the eye of any journalist – even in a story already packed with oddities – he later told Lloyd he spent that night at a bed and breakfast. Explaining his reasoning, he said: "It's been a long day for everyone and I could do with a bit of space now."

Almost two decades later, the origins of the siege remain somewhat baffling. Lloyd gathered that the man had shown the replica firearm to his partner's sixteen-year-old son, and this had somehow led to his neighbours calling the police. Armed officers arrived, but the man was inside the house and only became aware of them when they phoned to demand that he give himself up. He told Lloyd he wanted to get dressed and eat breakfast before surrendering – then "stubbornness" took over and a five-hour siege ensued.

And the story doesn't quite end there. As Lloyd told me this tale in March 2022, she Googled the man to check a detail about him – only to discover that he was jailed for murder in 2020. The killing had taken place in 2007 (two-and-a-half years after the fake-gun siege) but he was only caught after confessing to friends in 2019.

* * *

When the phone rang at the *Welwyn Hatfield Times* one day in March 2019, no one rushed to pick it up.

"If you need a story, you want to be first to the phone," said Mia Jankowicz. She had just walked away from her desk, not in desperate need of a story, but apparently no one else was either. "There was a slightly determined silence from everybody else, so I picked up."

The man on the line said: "I've got a story for you." These words do not inspire giddy optimism among seasoned reporters, who have often heard them followed by three-week-old news of a village bake sale. At first, the details of this call seemed fairly ordinary. The man's wife was about to turn sixty, and she was retiring from her job at the University of Hertfordshire on the same day.

"I thought it might work [as a small story] but he carried on to say 'and as a surprise for her leaving, I'm going to pick her up from work in a tank'. I was so glad I picked up the phone," Jankowicz said. With a little fact-checking, she found that the man had indeed rented a tank – or, to use military precision, an Abbott 433 Self-Propelled Gun – from a company called Tanks-Alot. She said she "got a bit nerdy" about the story, interviewing the boss of Tanks-Alot about the practicalities of tank travel – which include being exempt from MOT and road tax.

After speaking to Jankowicz, I couldn't resist visiting Tanks-Alot's website. On the page advertising an Abbott 433 for sale (£38,500 plus VAT if you're interested), it says: "Excellent for the school run and general shopping outings." Driving such a vehicle to school, the shops or your wife's retirement might not appeal to a shy person, but Jankowicz said the husband had a "definite sense of showmanship", which he demonstrated in that first phone conversation.

"How he presented the story was deliberately designed to bury the lead. He knew he had a brilliant hook at the end," she said. "The husband talked about various things he could do [for his wife's retirement]. He wanted this iconic image of his wife riding in a tank like Thatcher in the 1980s." He got his wish, and the paper ran the story and pictures of a happy – if slightly baffled – university employee leaving work in a 17.5-tonne armoured vehicle.

When the fun was over, Jankowicz said she put in a "sneaky call" to the police, just to ask: "Did you get any weird calls today?" She added: "I thought it would be a great story if people had called the police." But, rather surprisingly, no one had contacted the local constabulary to report a tank driving merrily along the streets of Hatfield.

Looking back, Jankowicz called this a "very special story" – but she stressed that less eye-catching tales are still important. "It's not to diss writing someone's sixtieth birthday or their retirement up, because there's always something really human about those stories – but you throw a tank in the picture and it's so much fun."

. . .

"Have you heard about the goat that was in the pubs in Horley at the weekend?"

Chris Madden knew he had a story when a caller said these words. It was 2011 and Madden, a trainee on the Gatwick and Horley edition of the *Surrey Mirror*, found himself calling a pub landlord to ask: "Did you have a goat in your pub?" The landlord said yes, but added that the goat and its temporary keepers were not there for long because goats were not allowed in his pub. A very sensible rule, albeit one that would rarely come into play.

"Two people had stolen a goat from a field and had taken it on a pub crawl round Horley," said Madden, who pieced the story together by talking to local contacts and the police. In one pub, a landlord told the visitors: "You can't have a dog in here." The amateur goatherds told him: "It's not a dog". Right on cue, the goat stuck its head up above the bar.

Their motives remain unknown, but it seems they gave up on their adventure after repeatedly being refused service. "It ended with them releasing the goat in the Jack Fairman, the big pub in the centre of town," Madden said. "I think the goat was found and returned to where it had come from." He added: "It's the most ridiculous front page I've ever done."

• • •

It might seem ridiculous to question the political leanings of a pair of slippers, but Jamie Buchan found himself doing just that after a Perth pensioner phoned him at the *Courier* in September 2017. Buchan had just returned from holiday. His news list was empty, but the caller provided a bizarre story.

"He phoned up and said something along the lines of 'I have just bought these slippers… and I'm disgusted to find they've got swastikas on the soles'. I nearly fell off my chair," Buchan said.

He told his colleagues "I've got to go and see these slippers" and – arriving at the man's house – he was "horrified and thrilled" to see a swastika pattern on the soles. That might sound an odd reaction, but all journalists know the thrill of finding something shocking – especially when nursing an empty news list.

Buchan said the man was genuinely upset, but also knew he had provided a strong story and was "quite happy to play along with us". Back at the office, Buchan got some push-back from an editor who couldn't see the swastika pattern. However, once Buchan circled the offending shapes using a photo editor, his superior relented and accepted that these were, indeed, extremely right-wing slippers.

"It's one of those things – once you see them [the swastikas in the pattern], you can't not see them," Buchan said. He contacted the manufacturer, who – presumably shocked themselves – gave the following statement: "This is the first time that this has been brought to our attention. This outsole is widely available in China and has not been developed by us." They added that the pattern was meant to be a "honeycomb maze" and (as Buchan summarised their comments) "nothing to do with the Third Reich".

Still, the purchaser remained unhappy with his new, possibly fascist, footwear. He told Buchan: "My father and three uncles fought in the war and that image is not something I want in my house."

During my time in local papers, which ended in 2013, local hacks could still phone national papers and try to sell a strong story to supplement their measly salary. By the time of Buchan's story in 2017, things moved much faster – less than an hour after his slipper story went online, national news websites had it too.

. . .

Many local journalists interviewed for this book told me that bizarre and ridiculous stories stick in their minds far more strongly than hard news about death and destruction. That's certainly true for me, and perhaps for Gabriel Shepard, who told me that – during his time as news editor at the *Kent and Sussex Courier* – "we reunited a ninety-five-year-old woman with a stolen scarecrow".

"It was one of those village scarecrow competitions," Shepard said. "At the local care home, they had made this Wile E. Coyote scarecrow." While this might seem somewhat odd, it's a mere side issue in this particular tale. The paper had run a piece about the competition, and Shepard said: "The next thing we knew, we had the care home on the phone saying their scarecrow had been stolen overnight."

So the *Courier* ran another story, this time telling a presumably bemused readership that – unlike his nemesis the Road Runner – Wile E. Coyote had been captured. Who had done it, or why, no one knew. The paper came out on a Friday and, just as the editorial staff prepared to clock off for the weekend, someone phoned and said: "I saw the picture in the paper and I've found the scarecrow."

OK, coats back on their pegs. Shepard sent a reporter to collect the scarecrow from the roadside where it had been discovered, and drive it to the care home. But it wasn't so simple.

"The scarecrow was massive, so it wouldn't fit in her car," he explained. "We tried to commandeer a van to get it down there. That didn't happen, so we ended up having to hide the scarecrow in the undergrowth over the course of the weekend." This allowed extra time to get the *Courier*'s van back from the repair garage.

"Luckily, no one stole the scarecrow over the weekend," Shepard said. A reporter collected it and took it to the care home, reuniting it with its owner in a happy moment for everyone concerned. Looking back, Shepard said the experience was: "Crazy, stupid local newspaper stuff – organising the logistics of a stolen scarecrow being returned to its owner."

. . .

If walk-ins and ring-ins are old news, posted letters sound like something from the Stone Age. But in 2015, the *Croydon Advertiser* received a letter from a woman who had been injured by a falling fence in Croydon town centre. Samantha Booth, who had joined as a reporter two months earlier, was sent to find out more. She arranged to visit the letter writer. Arriving at the house, she met a friendly couple in their seventies.

"They invited me in and made me a cup of tea," Booth said. As they chatted in the front room, which contained lots of family pictures, the man mentioned that his daughter had been murdered. Booth admits being "completely overwhelmed" by this unexpected turn in the conversation. The couple explained that their daughter, Lorraine Benson, had been murdered in 1988 at the age of twenty-two. Almost thirty years on, a parole hearing had raised the possibility of her killer, John Dunne, being moved to a low-security open prison. Booth stayed with them for a couple of hours, discussing their daughter – whose bedroom had been kept as it was in 1988 – and their fears over the pending parole decision.

"We just spoke about everything," Booth said. "I think it was nice for them to talk to somebody totally new. They were so kind to me. We have stayed in touch." The couple still wanted a story about the falling fence, so Booth wrote it up and the *Advertiser* published that first.

"Then the next week we ran the story about their daughter's killer," she said. Reflecting on how a letter about a fence turned into a story about a murder from three decades earlier, Booth added: "It just shows that literally anything can happen in this job."

CHAPTER NINE
On patch: Brothel knocking, Croydon Christmas & pirates hate Britney

WALK-INS AND RING-INS ARE GREAT (I've literally written a book about them) but even in the heyday of local papers, reporters couldn't simply wait for news to come to them. I once worked with a sub-editor who summed this up by describing a particular reporter as "more of a farmer than a hunter". Nail on the head. You need farmers, sure, but every editor wants some hunters too. There are countless ways to hunt for news and – in the old days, at least – it often meant going outside. This chapter will explore the delights of going "on patch" (leaving the office to look for news in the area you cover).

When I joined the *Crawley News*, the town's colour-coded neighbourhoods were neatly divided among the reporters – and woe betide any colleague who set a single toe in one of mine. But going out on patch isn't always easy. In the right mood, on the right day, it can be a goldmine. The sun shines, your notebook fills with immaculate shorthand, and you stroll back to the office in time for lunch. But if contacts and ideas dry up, and it won't stop raining, you can end up browsing community noticeboards like a reluctant child prodding unwanted vegetables around a plate. Just like bobby-on-the-beat policing, there's an art to finding stories on patch. Everyone has their own method, but it comes down to this: get people talking.

"I talk to everyone," said *Sunday Post* reporter Janet Boyle, summing up her approach. "Everyone has a story." Giving an example from 2013, Boyle said chatting to a fellow customer at a café in a "trendy and West Endy" part of Glasgow led to a story that made international headlines and featured on *Have I Got News For You*.

"She told me that she was a Merchant Navy officer and I asked if that took her around the world," Boyle said. "Did she ever encounter pirates off the Horn of Africa? How did she cope with threats of ambush?"

The sailor's reply was a gift-wrapped story: ships play Britney Spears music to scare pirates away. "Apparently they hate it, especially at such a high volume," Boyle said. The resulting story contained some lovely details, including which songs were most effective as pirate deterrents ("Baby One More Time" and "Oops! I Did It Again"). The sailor explained: "These guys can't stand Western culture or music, making Britney's hits perfect."

Leaving the café, Boyle said she was concerned the sailor's superiors would block the story. Far from it. The sailor even posed in her uniform with a Britney CD in one hand and her finger in her ear. In a marvellous quote from the British Association of Private Security Companies, a spokesman said loud pop music "has been proven as one of the most effective ways of fending off attackers", adding: "Each security company will have its own music choice."

Boyle admits her talk-to-everyone approach has got her into trouble at times. "My late dad was a fire fighter and one of his colleagues had his face burned," she said. "Out of politeness, no one ever mentioned it. So after mass one Sunday curiosity overcame me and I asked him exactly how it had happened. My parents were furious and told me to stop quizzing everyone. Guess I never learned."

· · ·

Getting people to speak can be tricky. As a breaking news reporter for the *Manchester Evening News*, James Holt often finds himself at the scene of death and destruction, approaching bystanders or going door to door for information. This can be unpleasant, he said, especially if he arrives soon after a tragic incident. People sometimes "assume that we are these bloodthirsty, awful people", he said, but he believes speaking to people makes an article much more human than simply reporting the basic facts.

In October 2022, while writing this book, I spotted a tweet from Holt and was instantly determined to include it. I contacted him, and he told me the full story. It began when he was sent door knocking on a wet, chilly evening in Sale, where a man had been killed by a falling tree.

"It seemed like a very tight community, so I was already a little bit wary of knocking on doors because it had only happened two hours before I got there," he said. Many people knew the man who had died. Devastated by the news, they were unwilling to speak. Doors were slammed in Holt's face – the "most hostility I've ever been met with at a scene" – and he was close to giving up. He decided to try one last door. The door in question contained a round glass window, and Holt saw a man inside.

"This guy started walking down the hallway," he said. "He looked at me as if he had seen a ghost. He looked absolutely mortified." Holt "sort of recognised him from somewhere" but could not place him, so he decided to "keep it professional" and go through his usual door-knock routine. He introduced himself and said he was from the *Manchester Evening News*.

"As soon as I said it, my ex-partner – who I was together with for a number of years – popped his head around the door just inside," Holt said. The penny dropped. The vaguely familiar man was his ex's new partner who, Holt now realised, must be concerned by the arrival of this unexpected visitor. In this unbelievably awkward situation, Holt led with "how are you?", apologised and quickly explained this was simply a weird coincidence.

"We all kind of stood there for a couple of seconds. I said 'this is a bit awkward'. We all laughed," Holt said. He was suddenly aware of being cold and wet – looking "like a drowned mole rat standing at the door" – while his ex and his new partner were probably enjoying a pleasant evening in.

As he trudged away, Holt recognised his ex-partner's car outside. If only he had noticed this before, he could have swerved this particular address. But no harm was done. His ex messaged to say a friend had heard about the tree falling and joked that Holt might turn up – and, incredibly, he had done. The surprised couple were "very very nice", Holt said.

"I look back and just think it was funny," he added. "Of all the houses in Greater Manchester, of all the millions of people who live in the region, it would be my luck to knock on that door." As he put it on Twitter: "Only I, JAMES HOLT could go to a scene and knock on a door… only to learn it is my ex's house where he lives with his partner when the door opens. I want the ground to swallow me."

* * *

In the mid 2010s, Charis Scott-Holm also fell victim to a weird coincidence while reporting on a serious incident. A kebab shop in Goole, East Yorkshire, had been broken into and set on fire – and the blaze had almost melted a mains gas pipe. Arriving at work at the *Goole Times* the next morning, Scott-Holm was sent to the scene, which happened to be one street along from where she lived.

She found the owner standing outside the shop, among wreckage that included various garden tools that had apparently been used by the intruders. Looking at the tools, Scott-Holm was stunned to realise they belonged to her. The last time she had seen them, they had been weighing down a tarpaulin in her garden. Now they were accessories to arson. Her wheelie bin – emblazoned with her address – was also present, having been dragged to the scene and used to climb over the shop's back fence. Deciding it was best to come clean, Scott-Holm told the takeaway owner that the tools and bin belonged to her.

"When I said 'I think those are mine' she was just so dumbfounded," Scott-Holm said. "The police turned up and I explained the situation." Her tools – including a mallet that had apparently been used to smash the shop's door – were bagged up as evidence and taken away.

Writing a front-page story about the fire, including quotes from the devastated owner, the editorial team decided not to mention their reporter's odd connection to the incident. Scott-Holm added: "The police gave us our tools back but they never found out who did it."

• • •

Like the elusive Goole arsonist, a young man in Bradford in the late 1980s was determined to evade the authorities. Facing deportation from the UK, the Sikh took sanctuary in his local temple. His plight was soon picked up by journalists, including Richard Horsman of *Pennine Radio*.

Horsman said the temple was unglamourous from

the outside – a converted building down a back street – but the inside was beautifully decorated. This was matched by the warm welcome he received on every visit.

The case had dragged on, leaving the man living in the temple for several weeks, so Horsman dropped in one day to see if there was an update. As always, the people at the temple were highly hospitable. But this time they insisted on giving him food and "endless cups of chai". Horsman said he wasn't allowed to progress beyond reception. When he asked to go in, he was offered more food and tea.

This went on for about twenty minutes. Horsman eventually spoke to the fugitive, but he left feeling convinced something was going on. Speaking to other journalists, his suspicion only grew. "When I compared notes with other guys on the same patch, they had very similar experiences," he said.

The truth soon emerged. "It transpired the guy got bored and was in the habit of going home to sleep in a nice warm bed, with his family around him," Horsman said. "It probably gets a bit boring in a temple if you sit in there, day in and day out." If journalists came knocking while the man was at home, the plan was to delay them while he was smuggled back into the temple. Horsman does not recall anyone running a story revealing this deception. He said it became a running joke among reporters, and there were no hard feelings. He believes the man was never deported. Perhaps the authorities think he's still in the temple.

• • •

Good local papers need open lines of communication with the public, so journalists should make themselves easy to find (professionally at least – don't give out your home address!). Even before the widespread closure of local newspaper offices, reporters were often sent to run drop-in sessions in the community, making sure readers could chew your ear off without having to get the bus to town. While Stuart Robinson (appeared in Chapter Three, lucky duck story) was at the *Yorkshire Evening Post*, this was called Meet Your Reporter.

"You know the drill, it was one of those bright ideas that management had every now and then to give us a presence in communities and reconnect us with readers," he said. "In actuality, what it involved was them taking the ancient red leather sofa from reception and plonking it in a shopping centre where the lucky reporter for a given patch would go and sit for a few hours and wait and see if anyone would come and speak to them. Moving from the sofa was not permitted."

On one Meet Your Reporter day, Robinson went to Cross Gates in Leeds. "I was accompanied by the paper's mascot, Scorch the Dog – a member of the advertising team dressed as a puppy in a T-shirt and baseball cap. I'm not kidding," he said. "As you can probably imagine, Meet Your Reporter was a massive poisoned chalice, not least because it would mean sitting there and either not doing anything for what seemed like an eternity or, worse still, being approached by people convinced they had an amazing story to tell but who almost invariably didn't. Anyway, on my day in Cross Gates, I sat for a good hour chatting with Scorch and doing pretty much bugger all else."

Robinson continued: "After a good while, I was approached by an older fellow who told me he was sick of the *Yorkshire Evening Post* not doing any stories about Scouts. After ten minutes or so... I eventually got a bit fed up and said that if he wanted us to do more stories on Scouts, he'd need to actually tell us something worth covering."

The man replied: "Well, you could do something on my Viking ship." Asked for more information, he added: "My Viking ship. I'm building it in the church hall for the Scouts, then we're going to burn it."

Forbidden to abandon his sofa, Robinson asked if he could go and see the ship once his shift was done. He expected to find "some terrible papier-mâché construction".

"Instead, I toddled up to the church and found a pretty spectacular, twelve-foot-long painted wooden longship in the church basement," he said. "Apparently the chap had been building them for years, and then the Scouts would take it out to their annual summer get-together and have a Viking celebration where they'd set it on fire. It made a page three and I think I was the only person to ever get something even half decent out of Meet Your Reporter."

. . .

A good reporter will grab a throwaway line about a Viking ship and pull until a story emerges. For Michael Connellan (appeared in Chapter Six, door kicker story), the word that leaped out of a sentence was "scythe". He was talking to a woman who he first met when her teenage son was convicted for helping to arrange a kidnapping. That might sound odd, but in local journalism (at the *Crawley News*, at least) odd was normal. Anyway, on this occasion the woman was on crutches. Sensing a possible story, Connellan asked why.

"She and someone else had together been cutting a hedge, both with scythes," Connellan said. Scythes? Really? OK, let's carry on. "The other person's scythe had slipped out of their hand whilst swinging it, curled through the air, and sliced through her [the woman now on crutches] Achilles tendon." Connellan wrote it up. Job done. But the woman wasn't finished making headlines: "A couple of years later, her nose was bitten off by her pet dog which she'd let sleep at the foot of her bed. I felt for her – and myself, as our rival paper got that interview first. I thought at the time that she was cursed. I look back now and think that tough things happen more often to people in tough, neglected towns."

Connellan wonders if it was right for journalists to persuade the town's citizens to publicly share their agonies. He's still not sure: "Sometimes yes, sometimes no." What he is sure about is that he – like many reporters – became a "magnet for chaos", sometimes getting embroiled in stories in the process of reporting them. One such instance happened when he was contacted by the wife of a man called Alan who been paralysed after a spinal infection.

"He was supposed to have an electric wheelchair

delivered to him by the local NHS trust shortly after he was discharged home from hospital," Connellan said. "But there were repeated delays to the wheelchair's arrival, meaning he was stuck lying on his back when his wife invited me over, propped up on pillows in a bed that they'd set up in their living room. He and his wife gave me some pretty heartbreaking quotes about how his paralysis, and then the health authority's inadequacy, was altering their lives. I was delighted, therefore, when a town resident saw my story and got in touch with me, saying that their recently deceased mum had left behind an electric wheelchair." Connellan helped the reader deliver the wheelchair to the paralysed man.

"Before long, he was in the garden in it, with his small children shouting 'you're clever daddy!' as he navigated left and right around the flower pots," Connellan said. "It was perfect: we as a newspaper had helped a community come together to help a father, whilst continuing to justifiably humiliate the local health authorities."

But there was a bitter sting in the tail. "I got in touch with the family again a little while later," Connellan explained. "Alan had died. The donated wheelchair, which wasn't the right fit for him, had exacerbated bedsores from hospital, which had got infected and killed him. Thinking back on this episode, it encapsulates journalism for me, in that I'm never sure if we made things better, made things worse, or made no difference at all."

This is an uncomfortable but essential issue for journalists to consider. Many of the examples in this book probably gave people some enjoyment, amusement and/or satisfaction. A few unequivocally made life better for one or more people. Having reflected on Connellan's words, my honest but unsatisfying conclusion is that journalists get involved in messy situations and rarely make them tidier. As with the case he highlighted, your involvement is usually short-lived, and you rarely have much influence over how things turn out. All you can do is an honest job. You play your part, and trust others to play theirs.

• • •

For all the difficult issues that journalism raises, it is often depicted as glamorous: reporters meet the rich and famous, grill MPs in the halls of Parliament, or fly with presidents on Air Force One. Local journalism is seldom like this. It can be thrilling, but most local reporters have done some variation of Meet Your Reporter, possibly with some variation of Scorch the

Dog. I certainly spent more time eating stale custard creams at evening council meetings than chatting up celebrities over champagne (in fact, I spent exactly zero time doing this).

Local journalists aren't motivated by such things – or, if they are, they made an astonishingly poor career choice. Still, it's sometimes nice to meet the great and/or good. I met various politicians, actors including Sir Patrick Stewart, and had an embarrassing encounter with a man I wrongly believed to be Sir Rod Stewart. I also spent a memorable day at Crawley's K2 leisure centre, interviewing sports stars involved in a reboot of the TV show *Superstars* including Dame Kelly Holmes, Sir Steve Redgrave and Roberto Di Matteo.

・ ・ ・

Celebrities on patch can be entertaining, although it's not always easy to turn it into local news (I believe I asked the *Superstars* athletes what they thought of Crawley's sports facilities).

The arrival of national news journalists – usually for a short period to cover a major story – is another matter. Suddenly your patch is awash with TV cameras and satellite trucks. Depending on the story, the nationals might offer money to secure exclusives, leaving you to read the news along with everyone else. But all those hard yards on patch – council meetings, community events, chatting to people at pubs and bus stops – can pay off here too.

For Dhruti Shah (appeared in Chapter Four, David Suchet story), this moment came during her time at the *Harrow Observer*. A local man, peace activist Norman Kember, had been freed after almost four months as a hostage in Iraq. Widespread media coverage had followed his capture in November 2005 by a group called the Swords of Righteousness Brigade. Inevitably, national and international media moved on, but Shah and her colleagues continued reporting.

Shah said local papers are more accountable to their readers, and have an obligation not just to report on such stories but to be supportive of the people involved. Kember belonged to a church a few minutes' walk from the *Observer*'s office. During his captivity, Shah attended some Sunday services there – "not being intrusive but just making sure they were familiar with who I was". She said the paper's existing role in the community, which included reporting on events at the church and other local religious groups, meant people trusted the *Observer*. "You become quite friendly with people that you're reporting on," she added.

When news broke in March 2006 that Kember had been released, Shah said the *Harrow Observer* team asked themselves: "What do we do and how do we compete with the national and international press?" She was determined to get an interview. "We had a bit of an advantage because we were there every day," she said.

Shah cancelled a day off to try to speak to Kember, and took the calculated risk of knocking on his door (the family had been bombarded by media requests). She didn't plan to push it if Kember refused to speak, but his wife recognised Shah from her attendance at church services and invited her in.

Kember was cagey and didn't want to talk about his captivity, but he spoke about his relief at being home. It was only the second interview he had given, after the *Baptist Times*. Though it was not a tell-all interview, Shah said her sensitive approach – reporting for a community that had worried about Kember – helped to build a relationship for future stories. And it meant the *Observer* had a story that the nationals didn't. Speaking to the *Press Gazette* at the time, Shah's editor said national papers can pay people to speak, while "the most we can do is offer them a coffee".

• • •

Local reporters could be forgiven for thinking they can't compete when the nationals are in town. Shah's story shows that not every story goes to the highest bidder, but sometimes it's truly hopeless.

That was the mood in the car as *Yorkshire Evening Post* reporter Adrian Troughton drove to Eric Cantona's house in May 1993. Sitting beside him, the photographer – showing the sunny optimism for which his profession is renowned – said: "This is a waste of time. He's not going to talk to us." Troughton wasn't so sure. As he put it: "You never know what you're going to get with a door knock".

The photographer's gloominess was perhaps understandable. Cantona, then at the peak of his footballing powers, had just helped Manchester United win the Premier League. He had left Leeds United six months earlier but still lived in Leeds and remained big news in the city. Arriving at the address at eight o'clock on the morning after Manchester United won the title, Troughton found the flamboyant Frenchman lived in an unremarkable semi-detached house. Cantona's wife answered the door and said Eric was in bed, but she would go and ask him. She disappeared for about five minutes, then Cantona appeared and gave an interview and even agreed to have his picture taken on the lawn.

The interview focussed on football matters, but Troughton recalls Cantona was suffering in Leeds – his house had been pelted with eggs and his car had been keyed. Cantona's behaviour on the pitch was controversial (he once jumped into the crowd to kick a fan), but he clearly had a softer side. "He was so polite and generous with his time," Troughton said.

However, Troughton's brushes with football hardmen of the 1990s did not all end so sweetly. In 1990, while working for a news agency, he was sent to Elland Road to catch Leeds United's players after training. His task was to ask Lee Chapman about his controversial recent transfer to the club. Troughton approached Chapman as the players walked from the nearby training ground to the stadium. He fired questions at Chapman, who just bounced a ball and ignored him. Then Chapman's teammate Vinnie Jones came over and used "industrial language" to encourage Troughton to focus on other stories.

• • •

Tackling tough guys is a job some reporters might drop on the nearest trainee "to help them learn" (the eventual lesson is to do the same to the next generation of trainees). But every reporter has to face uncomfortable situations from time to time. The next story began with a series of nerve-shredding door knocks, which in turn led to a walk-in – which is where we'll start.

In 2007, a man buzzed the door of the *Crawley News*, walked in and handed a letter to reporter Michael Connellan (who featured earlier in this chapter). "You must print this," the man said, tone and features solemn. "You must print the truth about the prostitutes and our kebabs." This might seem an odd (if highly newsworthy) statement but Connellan knew exactly what he meant.

"The previous week had seen me visit eight different brothels in different neighbourhoods throughout Crawley, for an investigation into the town's sex trade," Connellan explained. "I'd visit a property and make sure that sex was on offer for money. Then, in the time-honoured tradition of a journalist, I would make my excuses and leave, with the excuse being that I'd forgotten my wallet in my car and would be back shortly. It was a pretty bleak experience. Unsurprisingly, the sex workers all had the air of victims of exploitation rather than independent courtesan entrepreneurs. I wanted to expose this hidden side of the town and put pressure on the authorities to address it."

Connellan had researched the addresses on "dodgy websites and freesheet advertising newsletters" (this being just after the time when local papers routinely printed such adverts, somewhat undermining our moral authority to comment on it). He went quietly about his business, only knocking on the relevant doors.

"The final suspected brothel of the eight was up a flight of stairs, taking me directly above a kebab shop," Connellan said. "On the other side of the street was a school. That meant the location of this brothel, if confirmed, would give me licence to print the greatest phrase in local news: this sex den was 'within yards of a local school'. Sure enough, in the manky flat, I was offered sex at a price of £60 by two women with Eastern European accents who, for some reason, insisted they were Spanish. I left and went downstairs to the kebab shop. It was 3pm and I was the only person inside with three kebab guys. Did they know, I asked, about the brothel directly upstairs?"

"What?" they screamed. "They're whores?"

Recalling the situation fifteen years on, Connellan concluded: "Oh dear." He continued: "It turned out the kebab guys owned the whole property, upstairs and down, and were landlords of the women upstairs. They pushed past me, out of their front door, and up the stairs – thankfully without their kebab knives. They banged on the door of the upstairs flat. I then watched as the two women were turfed out and chased down the street, trying to decide if I'd just helped stamp out the local sex trade, or if I'd simply made two vulnerable people homeless."

Back at the office, Connellan wrote up the story, which made a front page and double-page spread inside, including a map showing how the sex trade sprawled across Crawley's neighbourhoods. "It was the talk of the town when we published," he said.

Which brings us back to the *Crawley News* office and the kebab shop owner standing over Connellan, letter in hand. The man said: "Lots of customers are walking in and teasing us, asking 'can I get a woman here as well as a doner kebab?' It's upsetting. We are a family business. Please print this letter that says we had no connection to what they were doing upstairs."

Connellan did as the man asked, then waited a while before making contact again. "I visited the kebab shop a couple of weeks later to ensure there were no hard feelings, and make sure I wasn't missing a follow-up story," he said. "They tried to give me a free chicken shish and Diet Coke as thanks for publishing the letter."

. . .

A year after Connellan's exposé, another *Crawley News* reporter stood outside one of the addresses named in his story. Was this still a brothel? The reporter didn't know. That was the mission: visit all eight brothels and find out which were still operating. Even for an experienced, confident journalist, this was an awkward task – requiring rapid assessment of whoever opened the door, then the right excuses, depending on whether each building was a brothel or simply a home (perhaps belonging to people already sick of strange, sweaty men shuffling up to their door).

The reporter was no seasoned pro. He was a trainee – an extremely nervous, awkward one, scared of a simple vox pop, let alone multiple sex dens. This reporter was, of course, me. I recall glancing back towards the car where Connellan waited to whisk me away if I needed to run. I already wanted to run, but I'd just rung the doorbell. Fear had taken over and, happily for my journalistic career, fear of failing outweighed all other terrors. Still, my legs twitched, ready to sprint away from Crawley, never to return. I could go back to pub work, I told myself.

The door opened. So did my mouth. A woman looked at me. I looked back, frozen. She wore a sort of medical uniform – not like a nurse, but maybe a physio or a dental hygienist. A question crashed into my brain: *What do prostitutes wear?* Why hadn't I asked Connellan that before setting off?

Time stretched and twisted. The woman's polite expression faded to confusion. Perhaps she wondered if I was ill, drugged or simply broken, lost and alone. If so, she was basically right. I think I managed to close my mouth, then chewed thin air for a moment before finally – finally – finding some words. Not good words, obviously, but words nonetheless. Lacking Connellan's lazy charm, I believe I said something like: "Is this the house where you... you know... where I... where people can get... no, it isn't, is it? No, I'd better..." And I left, skin burning like a freshly boiled lobster. I barely persuaded my legs to take turns as I staggered down the short path and back to the eternal bliss of a public Crawley street.

We visited the other seven addresses from the previous story too. I knocked on four doors, Connellan knocked on four (being the decent fellow he is, or perhaps from sympathy at my near-incontinent anxiety, he didn't stick the trainee with all eight). As well as confusing a perfectly law-abiding physio, pharmacist or whatever she was, two of my others were plainly not brothels. In these cases, I knocked and very non-sex-worker-looking people answered, and I calmly bellowed "wrong number" and fled. I was braver at the next one, and even got a quote from the householder: "I still have perverts knocking at my door."

At the last address, I quickly learned what a brothel looked like. The woman who answered the door was about fifty percent motherly, fifty percent nightclub bouncer. Looking past her, I saw the house contained almost no furniture – just open doors and, in every visible room, a bed and a small table bearing a roll of toilet paper. I'm not sure what the woman would have done if she realised what I was doing. Brothels have some kind of muscle nearby, right? No idea. Maybe that's only on TV. Happily, I couldn't have looked more like a twitchy, sex-starved oddball if I'd tried. I had been perfecting the act all day. My doorstep U-turn probably made perfect sense. I think the woman even smiled slightly as I shot away.

So ended my stint investigating Crawley's illicit sex industry. Almost. I saw that same woman in court a few months later, charged with keeping brothels used for prostitution (not sure what else one might keep them for). When she spotted me sitting in the press box, I'm sure she gave me the same knowing smile.

• • •

Connellan's brothel investigation demonstrates the importance of coming up with ideas and finding your own stories. In my later life at the BBC, this was called OJ (which turned out to mean "original journalism", not orange juice). Such stories often serve the public by revealing hidden truths about their local area. But originality is also essential for more practical reasons, such as filling pages (especially in less "newsy" patches) and dealing with annual fixtures like the dreaded Christmas features meeting.

When news editor Gabriel Shepard (appeared in Chapter Eight, stolen scarecrow story) moved from the *Kent and Sussex Courier* to the *Croydon Advertiser* in summer 2011, he was already thinking about Christmas. Keen to impress his new colleagues, he told them he had a "brilliant idea". And they agreed. In fact, they liked it so much they had tried (and not quite managed) to pull it off last Christmas. This wasn't the response Shepard had expected, but they agreed to make it work this year.

The plan was to make a Croydon version of "The Twelve Days Of Christmas", finding something local for each line of the song. Some were easy enough. Some were hard.

"It's all very well finding five gold rings from the local jeweller, but what do you do for a partridge in a pear tree?" Shepard said. Could they find a local gamekeeper? Not sure a dead bird would strike the right tone. Could they persuade Steve Coogan to visit Croydon in character as Alan Partridge? If so, great, but it seemed unlikely.

Shepard stressed that the feature was a team effort, but he solved the partridge problem. His brainwave was to find someone called Partridge and photograph them in a place called (checks map) Peartree Close in Sanderstead, South Croydon. This took some work and effort.

"We phoned up everyone who was called Partridge," Shepard said, adding that journalism makes you accustomed to odd conversations. Even so, this was particularly tricky, and a couple of people hung up. With Croydon's supply of Partridges running low, he finally got his Christmas miracle, in the form of a local charity volunteer called Sylvi Partridge. "I kind of managed to talk her round," he said. Partridge volunteered at a mental health charity, and Shepard suggested the *Advertiser* could promote the charity within the feature. She agreed.

The next problem was logistical. Partridge lived on the opposite side of town from Peartree Close, so photographer David Cook was sent to collect her. Cook took some tinsel to decorate the Peartree Close sign, Partridge brought a Santa glove puppet and, as Shepard put it: "The rest is history."

The feature also included a local belly dancing group (nine ladies dancing), a load of plumbers holding pipes (eleven pipers piping) and, my favourite, ten pub landlords jumping – with varying levels of athleticism – as lords a-leaping. Some of the verses were filled in classic local newspaper style: model swans a-swimming were placed on a "lake" that had formed in a Coulsdon car park, much to the annoyance of motorists (they were annoyed about the puddle, not the swans).

The double-page spread brimmed with local charities, businesses and schools (twelve drummers drumming was a school steel band). "It was an opportunity for local groups and businesses to have a bit of a shout-out in the paper," Shepard said.

And how was the feature received?

"I think, sadly, because it was Christmas week it was one of those weeks when people don't tend to buy the paper, so it was potentially missed by a few thousand readers," Shepard said.

But what of the woman who made it all possible? "I never heard back from Sylvi Partridge," he said. "I assume she was happy with it."

• • •

While local papers usually celebrate the birth of Christ by publishing quirky features, very few devote the same column inches to the son of Satan. OK, that's a weird sentence. Bear with me.

As the date approached 6 June 2006 (6/6/6), *Sevenoaks Chronicle* news editor Oliver Frankham had an idea. He knew that Harvey Stephens – who thirty years earlier played the boy Damien in the film *The Omen* – lived nearby. Frankham sent chief reporter Owen Morton to see what he was doing. Perhaps Stephens would be marking this occult occasion by holding a séance or sacrificing a goat in honour of the dark lord of the underworld.

No such luck. "I think he was having a quiet drink in the pub," Frankham said.

That edition of the *Sevenoaks Chronicle* might have been distinctly un-scary but – as described in chapter six – working as a local reporter can often be terrifying. For me, work-related fear wasn't about angry walk-ins or playing paparazzi outside courts. No, I saved my deepest dread for two particular jobs that will be explored in the next chapter: death knocks and vox pops.

CHAPTER TEN
Twin terrors: Death knocks & vox pops

WE NEED A NEW LAW. It should apply to anyone who commissions a vox pop (short for vox populi, or "voice of the people", it means hitting the streets and asking the public what they think about something). The law should be as follows: when sending a fellow human to conduct a vox pop, editors must provide them with a question or subject about which – in all reasonable probability – the general public will have an opinion. The punishment for breaking this law – Alex's law – shall be six months of compulsory attendance at evening meetings of the council's planning committee. Also a fine. And you have to buy everyone coffee.

Why do I care so deeply about this? Well, as any reporter will tell you, asking a stranger to give their opinion, name, age and – worst of all – be photographed or filmed, is hard graft. This is fair enough if you're asking their view of a controversial political issue. Which party leader do you prefer in tomorrow's general election? What do you think about the train drivers' strike? Do you support the plan for a new mega-casino in our village? All fine. You ask people. Some say no or simply ignore you. Others speak but refuse to have their picture taken (even though you labour the point about how small it will appear in print). And some give you what you need. They give their opinion and, if you're lucky, you get the required number of speakers, offering a range of views.

Even with a decent question on a decent subject, it can be tricky. For example, I went to Didcot for *BBC South* in 2013 to report on the closure and demolition of the town's coal power station. Didcot is in relatively flat Oxfordshire countryside and, as I remember it, the gigantic power plant literally loomed over it. And yet no one seemed at all bothered. The plant could keep belching out coal fumes, or be levelled by artillery bombardment – Didcot's population had no preference. Some seemed barely aware of its existence – to the point that, during one conversation with an apathetic local, I turned to look at the colossal cooling towers, gesturing vaguely in their direction and wondering if this was all a dream.

Still, with the exception of those baffled and baffling shoppers, most people would have a view on such a prominent local issue, or could at least be encouraged to form one. I chose to be a journalist, so I can't complain about being asked to speak to people about news. But all too often editors – perhaps repaying cruelty done to them in their own trainee days – make reporters extract opinions from people who simply don't have any. It's not the public's fault. Most people don't know or care about the 0.5% change in business rates, a three-foot extension of a no-parking zone, or plans for a new pot plant in the council's offices. I should state at this point that I had relatively kind news editors, who rarely sent me vox popping on such subjects. Not everyone is so lucky.

In the late 2000s, Kerra Maddern of the *Exeter Express and Echo* was given a truly brutal vox pop. The task was to get twenty people to give their view on whether Exeter should become a unitary authority.

"I'm not even sure why I was asked as I wasn't covering local politics then, just education," Maddern said. "It could possibly have been because it was a bank holiday or a Sunday, hence the need for so many people to fill a page." And it got worse. She had to take the pictures herself – meaning she couldn't rely on that magical assertive impatience many photographers use to "persuade" people to have their picture taken.

In an impressive display of grit, Maddern headed to the Tesco Extra car park and got the job done in about an hour. It would have taken me a week. "It actually wasn't as hard as I thought it was going to be," Maddern said. "I remember having to start quite a lot of the vox pops with an explanation of what was going on, ie intricacies of local government, but people seemed fairly willing to talk." She added: "Vox pops were usually given to people on work experience and they only had to get four or five people. I think the news editor was apologetic when he asked me to do it, probably something the editor got in his head we should do. It wasn't an especially electrifying local issue at the time."

• • •

A twenty-person vox pop on local administration might sound tricky, but Maddern's near-namesake Chris Madden (appeared in Chapter Eight, goat pub crawl story) can top that by an order of magnitude.

It was Christmas and Madden, a reporter at the *Surrey Mirror*, had got himself into a situation. He blames himself. It was, he said, "what I got for turning up unprepared" for the Christmas features meeting. Such meetings can be stressful. You sit around a table in an airless office – or at the pub, if you have that kind of editor – and listen while others offer their ideas.

Sometimes those ideas are so good – or yours so weak, or non-existent – that you panic as your turn approaches.

This was Madden's predicament – except that he did have one idea. Trouble was, the idea was wildly ambitious. Should he suggest it? Could he pull it off? Time ran out. His turn came and – unable to think of anything "sensible or better" – he blurted it out. The pitch was this: he could gauge local Christmas spirit by dressing up as an elf and offering to hug people.

He wasn't too worried. Ideas would significantly outnumber commissioned features, so his pitch probably wouldn't get used. But he said editor Deanne Blaylock decided it was "an excellent idea that should definitely be done".

"At this point I had probably got myself a reputation for doing ridiculous features," said Madden, whose previous efforts included dressing up as a pantomime dame. In the case of the elf feature, he wasn't sure whether Blaylock really liked the idea, or simply felt it would be "good for me to have to make one of my silly ideas work".

"About a week after this meeting, I found myself in Redhill high street in a full elf costume, offering free hugs to strangers," he said. Incredibly, the plan was to offer a hundred hugs in Redhill and another hundred in nearby Reigate, to see which town had more Christmas spirit (and less devotion to personal space). He did it in a day, for which I award him the Medal of Journalism (patent pending).

"I think Reigate had more Christmas spirit," Madden said, recalling a 67-62 victory for the town – and remarkably high uptake in both. "We had a couple of slightly weird moments," he continued. One came when the "entire staff of the Rush hairdresser" heard about the hugging elf and came out for a group hug.

Madden also recalled a moment when the photographer spotted a big, bald, bearded biker approaching and said: "Go and offer him a hug. He will probably punch you. It will make a great picture." With reckless bravery, Madden took up this challenge and prepared to intercept the man, who was walking and talking on his phone. After hearing Madden's request, the man said into the phone: "Hang on a second, mate, I've just got to hug an elf." After the hug, he patted Madden on the head, said "nice boy" and continued on his merry way.

• • •

While Madden's Christmas cheer persuaded people to hug him, reporters often face suspicion while doing a vox pop. Many people don't like being approached by strangers – possibly fearing they could be robbed or, worse, asked to give money to charity.

This is brilliantly illustrated by a recollection from Irene Kettle (appeared in Chapter Six, milk bottle threat story). During her time as editor of the *Colchester Gazette*, the idea of "random acts of kindness" emerged as a trend. This had become popular in the USA, but would it wash in Essex? She gave £50 to a "shy" reporter and told him to give it away – not as cash, but in gifts to strangers. The reporter chose to buy chocolates and flowers, and tried to hand them out.

The result? It took him an entire (presumably gruelling) day.

. . .

While some vox pops yield very little, others strike gold. In 2015, cameraman Martin Colley and reporter Stuart Flinders filmed a vox pop for *BBC North West Tonight* in Liverpool, ahead of a football match between Liverpool and Everton. Their mission was tricky – they had to ask people if they remembered a famous FA Cup game between the sides almost half a century earlier, in 1967.

As with any vox pop, Colley said some people "walk past you like you're a charity chugger", and this one had the added difficulty that anyone younger than fifty-five was unlikely to recall the game. After a slow start, Flinders pointed out an older gentleman, who looked about the right age. The man stopped to speak, and Colley recorded a short clip that has now been watched millions of times online.

Flinders asks the man: "I'm just wondering whether you remember the derby match in 1967 at Goodison, FA Cup fifth round, and it was shown on a big screen at Anfield at the same time. Do you remember it?"

The man replies: "Yeah I do, I played in it."

"Did you?" Flinders says, obviously surprised.

"I was the goalkeeper for Liverpool," says the man, one Tommy Lawrence, who played more than three hundred games for the club. He adds: "It was a great game, yes. Alan Ball scored the winner."

Colley said he and Flinders were stunned, adding: "He finished what he was saying and me and Stuart couldn't quite believe what he had said." As Lawrence began walking away, Colley and Flinders realised they should do more with this, so they tapped him on the shoulder and took his phone number. "Stuart and another cameraman went to his house and did a follow-up with him," Colley said.

He said that day's vox pop might never have been broadcast – he and Flinders were sent to see what they could get. He added: "Sometimes [vox pops] are useful, sometimes they're not and sometimes you get something like that."

• • •

Sometimes you get far more than an unexpected football legend. While doing a vox pop at a St Patrick's Day event, Ellen Beardmore (appeared in Chapter One and Chapter Six) met her future husband. I asked what the man did to make such a good impression. Beardmore replied: "Nothing, but I clearly did – as he remembered me when we met again in a bar a year later!"

And Sam Blackledge (appeared in Chapter Two, Jesus bruise story) got a surprising – and possibly unwelcome – ego boost while vox popping for ITV Westcountry. A well-spoken gentleman began by answering a question about the local area but quickly changed subject to focus on the reporter: "I live a couple of miles outside the village, so I can walk in every morning and browse around and talk to good-looking chaps like you. You're probably not on camera, so the ITV people don't realise what a handsome beast you are."

From his safe place off-camera, Blackledge replied: "That's all we need. Thanks very much. Appreciate your time." As the man walks off, he tells the camera operator: "Make sure the 'handsome beast' goes in."

• • •

If you would rather not accost the public to ask for their views on St Patrick's Day, or have them comment on your appearance, how would you feel about door-knocking the house of someone who has recently died? This job – the "death knock" – is a rite of passage for any local journalist, and most quickly develop a method to cope with it. I had a bad start, being chased away from a house by a grieving widow and her massive dog. My mistake had been to appear at the door with my notebook in hand – something I often did on ordinary stories, but never again on a death knock. The family felt I had assumed they would speak, and phoned my editor to complain this was "just another story" to me. It wasn't – I was terrified when I approached that door – but I understand the conclusions they drew.

With that experience always in mind (I vividly

remember sitting in the car afterwards, shaking too much to use the controls), I harnessed my natural shyness to approach death knocks gently, ready to be turned away. I would begin with an apology, and explain that we offered a tribute article about local people who had died. This was true – such stories were always positive. You can't defame the dead, but there seems little point in doing so unless they were a truly despicable villain. I remember one Crawley widow who asked: "Why would you want to write about my husband? He was a cunt." We didn't run that one.

My sheepish approach served me well. A surprising number of people invited me in, and seemed willing – even eager – to talk about the person who had died. The one that sticks with me was a young woman whose partner, a British soldier, had died in Afghanistan. The soldier had sent her an action figure to keep until he returned, and she held it as we spoke. I kept my eyes determinedly off it. Death knocks require tact and empathy, but you must remain professional – and something about this simple plastic toy made me want to cry. The soldier's mother spoke too. They invited me to the funeral – an incredibly moving day when all of Crawley seemed to stop.

The death story that still haunts me comes from my time as news editor of the *Dorking and Leatherhead*

Advertiser. I didn't even do the death knock. One of the perks of being an editor is that someone else has to do that. In this case, a reporter tried but no one answered. A teenage boy had died – a big story, especially in a small town like Dorking. We saw plenty of tributes on social media, along with a picture, but I disliked ripping quotes and pictures from Facebook. Aside from copyright issues, the local paper needs to do better than reprinting pages from social media.

The best we could get was a quote from the boy's aunt. I think she also provided the picture we used. Still, in sleepy Dorking this was an obvious front page. I went home on deadline day with a sinking feeling. As it turned out, my dread was justified. When the paper was published, I got a call from the boy's parents. I remember every second of it. They called me on speaker-phone from a car, both in tears, angry and upset with our coverage. They particularly objected to the "horrible" picture we had used. The image was a somewhat grainy shot of the boy wearing a tuxedo and bow tie. There was nothing obviously wrong with it – but they hated it, and they hated seeing his death "splashed all over" our front page. What could I say? I agreed with them. I was totally ashamed and – while hardened hacks might have shrugged it off in seconds – I still am.

For me, this experience demonstrates why local news is the best training ground for journalists: you're forced to face the people you write about (or at least they have your direct phone number). When I read cruel, gossipy journalism – usually but not exclusively about famous people – it strikes me that the writers must be confident they won't have to meet the people involved. National newspapers and broadcasters have large offices with security guards at the front desk. There are plenty of good reasons for this, of course, and I'm not advocating exposing national journalists to anyone who fancies wandering in. I covered national news for the BBC, and I was happy enough to work behind high walls. But I'm certain every journalist's work would be a little better, a little fairer, if they knew the doorbell might ring at any time.

• • •

While death knocks might be uncomfortable, especially for new reporters, Angela Lord points out that bereaved people vary greatly – and reporters must risk facing hostility in order to reach those who want to speak.

"For many people, laying bare their grief for all to see is the last thing they want to do," Lord said.

"Others feel the need to talk about what happened, simply for the sake of their sanity. It all depends on the circumstances and personalities involved. Sometimes there are reasons to speak out: to help in the hunt for the killer in a murder case, or as a warning to others, for instance in a death from a drugs overdose."

At the *Croydon Advertiser* in the 1980s, Lord covered two deaths of young people whose parents had very different reasons for speaking to her.

"The first was a teenager who had been stabbed on the street," she said. "His mother agreed to speak to me because she wanted to talk about her son, to make it personal, to give his life more meaning than just another statistic in the long line of victims of knife crime. Talking to the press gave her that opportunity. The second time I spoke to the family of a dead child, it was a high-profile murder case. Both parents felt a deep need to talk through what had happened and I was invited into their home, and later attended their daughter's funeral."

Lord added: "It's part of a news reporter's job to knock on that door, even at the risk of a hostile reception. It's a situation which calls for a tactful and sympathetic approach, and the acknowledgement that everyone deals with bereavement in their own way, whether that is silently and privately, or in sharing their pain with the world."

• • •

High-profile deaths affect entire communities, putting extra pressure on reporters. The local paper must get the story, but it's also vital to respect the grieving family. In 1983, Paul Burnell (appeared in Chapter Two, cowboy record story) of the *West Lancashire Evening Gazette* found himself reporting on a major national story, after three police officers drowned while trying to rescue a man from the sea off Blackpool. A fourth officer's life was saved by a doctor who happened to be there.

Burnell – then a young reporter fresh out of school – was sent to the home of one of the officers who had died. Approaching the house, he saw a police helmet in the window. Nerves got the better of him and he admits he "bottled it". He added: "My dad was in the police and it was far too close to home for me." He tried a "gentle knock and hoped no one would answer it", then left. "I was in total fear for days on end that someone else would have got the story," he said.

This fear of being "scooped" – beaten to a story – haunts all journalists. This might be even more acute at local level, especially in the old days of print-first journalism, when you couldn't catch up by rushing a story on to your website. During my time in Crawley, the town's two papers – the *News* and the *Observer* – both came out on Wednesdays. So, if the town hall had collapsed and we had somehow failed to notice, this would be very obvious to anyone who saw the two papers. I recall a couple of Wednesday mornings when the *Obby* had scooped us, and the mood in the *News* office was pretty grim.

. . .

While Burnell was reluctant to intrude on a family's grief – even at the risk of being scooped – Tony Earnshaw (appeared in Chapter Six, cupboard hiding story) was baffled on one death knock to meet a "very jolly lady" who invited him in. It was the mid-1990s, and he had been sent to the address after the police released details of a man who had been killed in a road accident. Earnshaw quickly realised that the woman, the dead man's wife, was unaware of what had happened.

"I made an excuse… and left the house without explaining why I had called," Earnshaw said. "Then I sat in my car wondering what to do. Literally minutes later, a police car drew up, two officers got out and went into the house. They were there to deliver the bad news."

Earnshaw, then at the *Yorkshire Post*, called the newsdesk and asked what he should do. Incredibly (to me at least – maybe harder-nosed hacks will disagree), he was told to wait until the police left and knock again. He did as he was told. The woman answered the door again, looking "utterly shattered".

"Never forgotten it," Earnshaw said. "She spoke, but I felt lower than a snake's belly. The conversation was brief. And no collected pics. I legged it. Just couldn't look her in the face."

. . .

Kirsty McIntosh experienced this situation in reverse while working for Scottish regional paper the *Courier*: she phoned the family of a missing girl, not knowing they had just heard she was dead. The girl had been missing for two days, and McIntosh got the father's number and called him.

"He put the phone down on me," she said. "So far, so normal, but I did wonder why he'd turn down the chance to make an appeal. That afternoon we got the police press release saying she'd been found dead that morning, shortly before I'd called [the] dad. I still remember that girl's face. She would have been twenty-one this year (2022)." McIntosh added: "I felt awful. She's one of several story subjects I think of often. People think we're cold hearted, but these things stick with us all."

• • •

For some people, experiences like this prove fatal for their love of journalism. Jeff Wright was a photographer for the *Evening Mail* in Hounslow in March 1974 when news broke that a Turkish Airlines plane had crashed near Paris, killing all 346 people on board.

"As usual, the question was asked: anyone local killed?" Wright said. "There was. Reporter Joan Finlay and I were sent to see the family. The 'death knock'. Although I must say that I don't ever remember anyone using that term back then. We knocked. The door was answered and Joan explained we were from the local paper and would like to know about the victim. The grieving family let us in and Joan expertly asked the family questions about the husband's life and story. I asked to take a photograph of the family in their front room and they agreed.

"Then came the inevitable last question: do you have a picture we can use of the deceased? It went very quiet in the room while a photograph was found. During this heavy silence, the wife turned to us and said: 'you must find this a very hard and upsetting thing to have to do in your job'. Joan and I looked at each other. Neither of us spoke. And not a lot was said in the car back to the office. There was certainly no feeling of success that we had got in, got a story and got pictures."

Wright continued: "For me, this was a damascene moment. Such stories were rare but any similar job I was sent on, it didn't take much for the reporter and I to agree on the strategy to tell the desk: there was no answer, no one opened the door and the neighbours didn't want to talk. Later that year I applied to go to university as a mature student and left newspapers the following year."

CHAPTER ELEVEN
Out of office: Doors shut, DMs open

WHEN I JOINED THE *Crawley News*, I don't think we had a website. If we did, it was very much an afterthought. The *News* was a Wednesday weekly paper, and all our effort went into that. This included concealing exclusives from those scallywags (perfectly nice people) at the *Crawley Observer*, which was also a Wednesday weekly. So, if we unearthed a great story after deadline on a Tuesday, we had to keep it quiet for a full week.

Today, keeping a story quiet for a full minute is probably a sacking offence in half the newsrooms in the country. In the quest for clicks, some local news websites seem to publish half-formed nibs with the word "EXCLUSIVE" hammered in front of the headline. There is, of course, excellent online local news too – and some of that features later in this chapter. But back in Crawley, in what now seems like the early Jurassic period but was in fact 2007, rushing a story online simply wasn't a thing.

Online news did not arrive as a triumphant, ready-to-use replacement for silly old paper. It sidled in at first, like an awkward teenager on work experience who sits in the corner for half the morning before anyone realises he's there. I don't remember when we started putting stories online, but I recall staring in wonder when we first got a hundred views on an article. This was the early 2010s at the *Dorking and Leatherhead* Advertiser, which then sold about 10,000 copies a week. *Still*, I thought, *well done little website. Cute.*

We had teething problems. For example, our software was somewhat prudish, refusing to allow swearing of any sort. This included letters that formed swear words within longer words, so when we mentioned Scunthorpe United Football Club, the website helpfully changed it to S****horpe. I genuinely enjoyed dealing with the complaints about that one.

Even once we switched off the website's ability to auto-censor our journalism, the early iterations of the site looked like a badly subbed page of classified adverts. Headlines lay strewn across the screen, all the same size, accompanied by tiny pictures that must have forced readers to touch their noses to the screen. We also lacked basic controls, such as the ability to put the stories in order. New posts simply pushed the rest down – so if we broke the news of an alien invasion two minutes before posting a nib about a three-legged cat winning second prize at a village fete, Hattrick the cat would sit proudly atop the home page.

By the time I left local newspapers in 2013, things were changing fast. Local news websites were still fairly basic, but the direction of travel was clear. The journey has been remarkably fast. A decade ago, it would have been hard to imagine a story that appeared on journalism website *Hold The Front Page* in March 2022, just after I started writing this book. It said journalists at Reach PLC – Britain's biggest local newspaper publisher – would get "benchmark" click targets for their stories. Reach journalists would be required to increase their monthly page views by 40% by July, and 70% by the end of the year, with targets ranging from 80,000 to 850,000 views, depending on the publication and worker's role.

The article also cited Reach documents that warned of "consequences" for staff not hitting the July and end-of-year goals. Reach told staff that the scheme, entitled Accelerated Personal Development, was "not designed to be punitive" and the aforementioned consequences would "depend on the individual circumstances". Leaving aside the Orwellian abomination that is Accelerated Personal Development, Reach is hardly an outlier here. Several of the journalists interviewed for this book described an intense focus from management on click numbers – including a live "leaderboard" displayed in the newsroom. The result: everyone wanted to write traffic news and stories about extreme weather, as these are sure to get clicks.

And this issue isn't limited to commercial publishers. At the BBC – free from pressure to generate advertising revenue – we closely watched the stats. Unpopular stories soon sank down the news index into oblivion. Simply knowing what your audience likes, and doesn't like, inevitably affects your decisions. This comes with many benefits, but it creates a dangerous incentive to churn out "clickbait" – entertaining your audience, but perhaps not informing and educating them. I'm acutely aware that these goals – to educate and inform – sound pretentious. Good. We need some lofty ambitions. Journalists *should* educate their audience. Everything else is junk food – enjoyable, safe in moderation, but no basis for a balanced diet.

In the bygone era of print-first journalism, newspapers needed a strong splash. Failure to provide one affected sales. But these figures didn't arrive instantly. A front-page story couldn't be ditched after publication in favour of something about *Love Island*. In retrospect, that was wonderful. You chose your splash and hoped for the best. Sometimes you chose something worthy, aware that – as journalists learn in media law training – public interest and what interests the public aren't always the same thing.

However, it's easy to idealise the good old days. The impacts of the digital revolution are complex. As this chapter will show, the internet hasn't only crushed the old ways of doing things. There are countless new options for creative, determined reporters to find and tell stories. Some are using this for public-interest journalism, local democracy reporting and hyper-local news. And, while newspaper offices have been swept away by the online tide, the public (or at least the internet-savvy public) have countless new ways to contact journalists. So – leaving nostalgia aside – is it possible that the old-fashioned walk-in has simply gone digital? And could proper local journalism be ready for a comeback?

. . .

Kirsty McIntosh (appeared in Chapter Ten, missing girl story) considers herself one of the first "digital natives". Starting out as a journalist in 2010, she has used social media to find stories from day one. She joined the *Courier* in 2012, covering Perth, and she said walk-ins were still common at the time. But – somewhat unusually – these were handled by "old-school reporters". Being new, young and female, she said many walk-ins "didn't want to speak to me". She needed other sources of news, and social media was the obvious choice.

"For me, it's a really natural way to find stories, just because of the age I am," McIntosh said. At first, this approach – which involved a lot of time at a computer – was frowned upon in the office. As a news editor myself in the same period, I admit I felt suspicious of reporters who sat gazing at a screen when we needed stories. I also admit that when chief reporter Sam Blackledge explained Twitter to me, I thought it was boring, complicated and unlikely to catch on. But McIntosh, Blackledge and countless others found stories, many of which were as weird and wonderful as any walk-in.

McIntosh spotted a brutally honest Facebook advert offering a "horrendous car" that "stinks of mackerel". The ad continued: "Decent stereo, but I'm keeping that. I can get £90 at the scrappies for it so if [you] offer me more, you can have it." Reporting such stories isn't simply a case of lifting material from social media, McIntosh said. She called that "bad form" and said journalists should always contact people to find out more and check the facts. "You get so much more information if you actually speak to people," she said. In this case, the man gave an interview and even agreed to be pictured in his car, eating mackerel out of a tin.

Local Facebook pages offer easy links to people and communities, McIntosh said, and this helped her cover a large geographical area. She joined numerous groups, and the effort led to headlines including: "Owner grumpy after prized dwarf disappears from Perth garden." The stone ornament in question – Happy, from *Snow White and the Seven Dwarfs* – had been carved on commission and could not be replaced because the artist had since died. The owner said any replacement wouldn't have the same expression, adding: "Somehow *Snow White and the Six Dwarfs* doesn't sound the same." Happily for Happy and his (temporarily) unhappy owner, the statue was located and returned to its rightful place.

McIntosh's extensive portfolio of Facebook stories also includes a teacher who shaped a snowman to look like Darth Vader, and a woman who was filmed pushing a lorry up a snow-covered street single-handed. There's also the tale of the missing parrot, which provides a classic example of why you should always interview people if possible. The Facebook post simply appealed for help to find the wayward bird. But when McIntosh phoned the owner, he casually told her: "Oh, he thinks he's a pigeon." The conversation also revealed that the parrot had a swearing problem, and any potential rescuer was likely to be told: "You're a dick."

Online newsgathering was already integral to McIntosh's way of working before Covid-19, but she said the pandemic increased the amount of material being posted online – while of course making face-to-face contact much rarer. She stressed the importance of new sources of stories, such as TikTok (I guess this reference may not age well – like telling journalists to join MySpace), and said traditional media organisations have often been too slow to embrace these.

Since switching to the role of court reporter, McIntosh's use of social media has changed. Scouring local pages for news is no longer the priority, but she said the digital walk-in can still be a powerful tool. Comments on her stories – both on the *Courier*'s website and social media channels – can offer opportunities to expand on court stories. For example, a rape survivor commented on a story, and this led to an interview. McIntosh said: "She wanted to educate girls about all the relationship red flags, so that they didn't get into the same situation that she did."

Commenting on the new world of local journalism

created by the internet, and social media in particular, McIntosh said: "It does make the job much more 24/7. It intrudes into your life much more than a traditional walk-in would have." This has benefits – a message or even casual browsing can provide a good story for the next day. But spotting stories at two in the morning – or even receiving abuse about something you've written – blurs the lines between work and home. "You never switch off," she said.

• • •

Richard Duggan had switched off for the day – or so he thought. It was August 2017 and Duggan, then a trainee reporter at *Essex Live*, was browsing the dating app Grindr. "I remember being on the app one night and just seeing this face and thinking 'why do I recognise that person?'" he said. As he clicked on the profile, the penny dropped – the picture showed Quhey Saunders, who had died two months earlier. Saunders had been killed at a motorway service station. Duggan had covered the case, and a suspect was due in court soon.

So why would someone use the dead man's picture on a dating profile? The Grindr account carried no details except an age: twenty-two (Saunders was twenty when he died). There was little else to go on. Duggan lived in Chelmsford at the time, and geodata from Grindr showed him the profile belonged to someone about five miles away. He took a screenshot and showed it to colleagues at the news meeting the next morning. By then, the profile seemed to have disappeared – or, at least, Duggan couldn't find it. He never found out who had set up the profile, or why. "I suppose it was just some sick catfish (using a fake identity to trick people in online dating)," Duggan said.

While this story came from an unexpected source, Duggan said online methods including Tweetdeck and local Facebook groups are good sources of stories. He called the closure of newspaper offices a "sad reality" but said journalists can combine online newsgathering with old-fashioned methods to ensure they know what's happening in their area. "The best journalists I know at a local and regional level still ring their contacts every day," he said.

• • •

Despite the pitfalls, online dating can be wonderful. Possibly a bit too wonderful, in the case of a story covered in 2008 by Sandish Shoker, then a trainee reporter at the *Coventry Times*.

"A colleague spotted a story in the *Sun* about a woman who had abandoned her children in Florida and moved to Coventry to start a new life as a romance writer with a man she had met online," Shoker said. OK. Quite a lot to take in there. Headline could be a challenge. But let's not get ahead of ourselves.

The woman – who had been called Sandra Gebert in the USA but had now remarried and changed her name to Sandee McCann – had left Florida seven years earlier, and her family had not heard from her since. Now it seemed she was in Coventry, so Shoker's editor told her to track McCann down.

"So me and the photographer scoured the directory and drove around Coventry door-knocking at the address of every Sandra or Sandee McCann we could find," Shoker said. "After about three or four hours, we were ready to give up but we had one or two more left on the list. We knocked on the door of a house in a quiet street and we found her. She was no doubt a bit startled to see us on her doorstep but she let us in."

McCann gave her side of the story, which made the front page with the headline: "Will the real Sandee McCann please stand up?" And Shoker said the surreal tale didn't end there. "A week later I got a call from Sandee, who said a reporter from *ABC News* was at her door," she said. "She didn't want to talk to any other press so asked if I would speak to them and so I was interviewed for a piece on *Good Morning America*."

ABC's story included quotes from two of McCann's six children, who had thought their mother was going to London for a short holiday – not to start a new life in Coventry. It has no quotes from McCann herself. As the online story puts it: "McCann has refused public comment except for one interview with a small British weekly, the *Coventry Times*."

• • •

A few miles south of Coventry in 2010, Kevin Unitt wrote an unusual story for the *Leamington Observer* that soon spread far and wide. An acquaintance posted on Facebook, saying she had been asked to produce ID to buy a slice of quiche in Tesco. It seemed a zealous checkout worker believed the store's strict ID policy applied to "quiche bought over the counter" (as opposed, presumably, to quiche prescribed by a medical professional).

Unitt messaged the unhappy shopper, who gave him more details for a story. Tesco commented too, saying it had been unable to find the staff member who went rogue with a new quiche-ID policy. The Tesco spokesman added: "We're completely baffled how, or why, this has happened."

Thinking the tale might work for the nationals, Unitt offered it to the *Sun*, but they said no. That seemed like the end of the story, but Unitt said a press agency "tracked the woman down to her home, slightly repackaged my story and then sold it on themselves to the nationals". He said their process was "quite underhand", and his Facebook friend didn't like all the attention it generated. Writing a piece for *Hold The Front Page* at the time, Unitt explained that the widespread coverage attracted hundreds of comments.

"Some treated it for what it was – a funny story," he wrote. "One person in New Zealand said she 'lived in fear of quiche-wielding hoodies', while another reader suggested quiche was a 'gateway to harder stuff like Cornish pasties and pork pies'. But others began to deconstruct and take the fun out, blaming it on everything from New Labour and the 'PC Brigade' to big corporations mentally preparing us for the introduction of national identity cards."

The national and international coverage grew, and the woman who had been asked for ID changed her name on social media "due to random friend requests and seedy messages". She told the *Leamington Observer*: "I really want all this to stop now. It's quite scary when you read all the comments about you. It was supposed to just be a funny story!"

• • •

Ben Falconer spotted a funny story on a Facebook community group, where someone posted to ask if anyone in Nailsworth, Gloucestershire, had seen a Nissan Micra being driven across a common "luring the cattle with carrots". Not wanting to copy-paste a story from Facebook, Falconer contacted the lady who wrote the post, then spoke to the hayward (who looks after grazing animals on the commons). "I also sought permission from the group admins to use the content of the post. Plundering closed groups for content isn't on," Falconer said.

His story told of a "bizarre and dangerous chase" in which three elderly people were seen careering across Minchinhampton Common. A bemused local person said: "They were literally off-roading in a Micra and the boot was open with this woman sat in there, laughing and holding carrots out for the cows... the cows chased as the car drove over the grass." The story described the common's animal inhabitants as: "Around three hundred cattle, a small number of horses and a donkey called Alfie." Commenting on the strange treatment of the cows, the hayward told

Falconer: "They like carrots but this is a very curious incident. I am going up there but I am told they have gone now."

Falconer added: "I was about to go home when this story 'broke' so I posted it up quickly, so quickly that my colleague's byline was on it! Nowadays that would cost me dearly if I was still a reporter because the story went viral, recording huge viewing figures." This online popularity was boosted by the story being posted on the social media channels of *Angry People in Local Newspapers*. And the tale later appeared on TV, in the missing words round on *Have I Got News for You*. "Unsurprisingly, the panel failed to guess the headline," Falconer said.

"As a postscript to this, after I had left twenty years of local journalism behind, I was told the identity of the 'Micra Three' and now it all makes sense," he said. "But I am sworn to secrecy. I do see the Micra out and about now and again, though."

• • •

A striking lack of secrecy allowed Isaac Ashe (appeared in Chapter Two, BDSM bed story) to discover a surprising situation in 2012. As a reporter for the *Loughborough Echo*, he tracked mentions of the town on Twitter – and someone had posted to say they were heading up on the train to "do some filming".

"Didn't take much research to see what line of filmmaking they were in," Ashe said. He followed the train journey of the filmmakers, who then posted a picture of themselves outside a pornography studio on a Loughborough industrial estate. "I managed to work out where it was from the rooftops and Google Street View. So me and another reporter went down to knock," Ashe said. "The windows were all steamed up and there was a skip with a mattress in outside." Someone answered the door and – in response to the reporters' questions – simply said: "No idea".

But the gift of social media kept on giving. Ashe explained: "The actress then posted something about heading to do some filming on iPhones at B&Q. I rang the store up and interviewed the manager about it. He said he remembered them, as they went in the toilets for quite some time and 'didn't seem to be buying much'." The resulting splash sported the headline: "Cheeky porn stars film scene 'in B&Q toilet'."

Many of those who lived through the rapid decline of walk-ins have mixed feelings about the effects. Ashe misses the days of unexpected knocks at the door, but he accepts it was not perfect. He worked in one office situated near the local court, which led to some necessary defensive measures. "We had bars on the downstairs windows, and sometimes people from court would sit in the graveyard opposite the office staring at you," he said. Despite the loss of those good – and sometimes terrifying – old days, Ashe said the spirit of local journalism hasn't dulled.

"People still get in touch, and the weird stories are still important to our readers," he said. On the day I interviewed Ashe, his readers were equally interested (according to story stats) in a police cordon at Leicester Cathedral and a man who had complained about a cold McDonald's breakfast. "If that stuff wasn't part of the job, I wouldn't want to do it anymore," Ashe said. "You never know what you're going to be writing about."

• • •

The internet is clearly a good way to find modern stories about modern people using modern tech to do modern stuff. But online methods can also turn up tales from long ago.

In 2017, Victoria Temple became the *Gloucester Citizen*'s unofficial "gorilla correspondent". This might seem like an unlikely thing for a UK newspaper to need, but an unexpected find on a local Facebook history page made it happen. Temple – who called herself a "magpie for newsy things" – spotted a black-and-white picture of a gorilla sitting among a group of schoolchildren. "The comments beneath were really intriguing," she said. These included someone who wrote: "My granny remembered the gorilla."

John Daniel the gorilla with children in Uley.
Credit: the Uley Society

The image was apparently taken in a village called Uley, so Temple phoned a local contact, who put her in touch with village archivist Margaret Groom. Temple stressed that she was not the first to discover the story – it had been well-known and documented before. "But it was a story that had largely been forgotten, so I resurrected it," she said. And it was well worth resurrecting.

The gorilla had been captured as a baby in Gabon, bought by Major Rupert Penny and transported to the UK in 1917, arriving in Uley later that year. Given the name John Daniel, it attended the local school, took walks around the village and was known to drink cider and eat roses from people's gardens. Alyse Cunningham, Major Penny's daughter, even took John Daniel to dinner parties at her London home.

Eventually, caring for a growing gorilla became too difficult, and John Daniel was sold to an American, and later to the Barnum and Bailey Circus. But his health deteriorated, and the following message was sent to Miss Cunningham: "John Daniel pining and grieving for you. Can you not come at once? Needless to say we will deem it a privilege to pay all your expense. Answer at once." Miss Cunningham set off immediately, but John Daniel died of pneumonia before she arrived. The body was given to the American Museum of Natural History, where it remains on display.

Although she initially found the story on Facebook, Temple said she always tried to dig deeper. Readers would notice "if you just use their Facebook chat group for a story," she added. After her story on John Daniel was published, national newspapers picked it up, and she was interviewed on the *BBC World Service*.

And – in her new role as gorilla correspondent – she even found a follow-up (some achievement in what I assume is a largely gorilla-free part of Gloucestershire). In a section of her brain she thinks of as "weird facts about people in Gloucestershire", Temple recalled that a local wildlife expert had worked with primatologist Dian Fossey in Rwanda forty years earlier, and had trained Sigourney Weaver to grunt for the film *Gorillas in the Mist*. Temple said: "I rang him up and did a great follow-up feature… about the difficulties of raising a baby gorilla in rural Gloucestershire."

. . .

Looking back just a hundred years, the world is barely recognisable – yet we tend to assume the future will be much like the present, perhaps with incremental change along existing lines. In journalism, that means we expect fewer offices, fewer journalists, less-face-to-face interaction. But reality isn't so predictable. In the process of writing this book, it became very clear that journalists still yearn to see people and tell their stories. Given the opportunity, I suspect the public would prefer this too. In a few places, that opportunity is coming back.

In Govanhill, Glasgow, a bright yellow sign over a shop window declares: "Everybody has a story… what's yours?" Far from being a shut-down newspaper office, soon to become a betting shop or takeaway, this place is new. It opened in 2022, swimming directly against the tide of office closures. Called the Community Newsroom, it houses two publications: *Greater Govanhill*, a free community magazine, and *The Ferret*, which describes itself as "Scotland's investigative news and fact-checking co-op".

"It seems almost radical to be doing this, when actually it's just a return to what used to happen," said Rhiannon Davies, founder and editor of *Greater Govanhill* magazine. "It's interesting being in an office with people popping in to say hi," she said. "So much journalism on social media can be journalists talking to other journalists or other people who are already engaged." By contrast, *Greater Govanhill* aims to provide a "platform for marginalised voices to tell their stories in their own words", avoiding both sensationalism and an "exploitative approach to personal stories". Instead of feeding into negative narratives about the area, the magazine takes a "solutions-focused approach".

As Davies put it, *Greater Govanhill* is "by the

community, for the community", supported by a membership scheme in which local people make a monthly contribution. She is under no illusions about the scale of the challenge, but when we spoke in January 2023 – a few weeks after the office opened – early signs were promising. "We're starting to get people bringing in issues to us," she said. "We're really keen to open it up. Next week we're starting to hold events to discuss local issues." Then, wonderfully, our call was interrupted by a walk-in. Returning to the phone after speaking to the visitor, Davies said: "The door is open. People can come in whenever they want."

• • •

"We are trying to take papers back to what they originally were," said James Cracknell, editor of the *Enfield Dispatch* – one of three North London papers run by community interest company Social Spider. "They [traditional papers] were launched in towns across the country as independent businesses, small-scale, with a local office and local reporters, trying to do the honest job of reporting what's happening in the local area."

Like many places, Enfield had thriving local papers until relatively recently. In chapter four, Martin

Beckford described his time at the *Enfield Gazette* in the early 2000s – and mentioned a rivalry with the *Enfield Independent*. In 2017, Beckford's old paper (by then called the *Enfield Gazette & Advertiser*) shut down. Meanwhile the *Enfield Independent* – run by Newsquest, the UK's second-largest local newspaper group – had lost its office and Enfield-based reporters, becoming what Cracknell called a "pretty poor imitation of what a newspaper should be". Social Spider already had papers in Tottenham and Waltham Forest, so Cracknell – who lives in Enfield – suggested setting up a new paper there. The *Enfield Dispatch* opened in 2018.

Cracknell spoke frankly about the difficulties the *Dispatch* faces. Due to limited funds, the paper is only printed monthly. It has few staff, so Cracknell does a variety of jobs including news editing, social media, running the website and writing newsletters. He even delivers stacks of newspapers (the paper is given out free at locations including libraries). "In some ways, my career hasn't moved on from when I was a paperboy at the age of thirteen," he said.

"Broadly speaking, we break even but we're not able to expand," Cracknell continued. He admitted finding the situation frustrating, but added: "I'm running a newspaper that has been able to close some of the gap of what was lost. That motivates me." All revenue is reinvested with the aim of providing a functioning local paper. "We are always trying to find ways to generate more money and use that to generate more journalism that we can put in people's hands," Cracknell said. He contrasted this with the "extraction" model of the large companies that own most UK local papers; the profits of such companies go to shareholders, while the *Dispatch*'s income stays in Enfield.

Cracknell said many community news projects depend heavily on a single key person, as the *Dispatch* depends on him. His goal is to make the paper self-sustaining, so – like a traditional local paper – it could carry on if he left. Despite the obstacles, the paper is making progress towards this goal. Two hundred of the *Dispatch's* readers support it with monthly donations. It now has one full-time reporter via the Local Democracy Reporting Service, through which the BBC funds local reporters and shares the stories they produce. The scheme's website says news organisations awarded these contracts must meet stringent criteria including "financial standing and a strong track record of relevant journalism". So, winning this contract from Newsquest in 2021 was a major boost for the *Dispatch*.

The next big step would be winning the contract to print public notices for the local council. Cracknell said this now provides the biggest income for some papers, but he faces a chicken-and-egg problem: the council can't give the contract to a monthly paper, and the *Dispatch* can't print more regularly without extra money. Winning that contract would be a major victory, and each victory strengthens Cracknell's optimism and resolve. The paper even has an office. It's a small room in a shared office building and, while walk-ins are rare, they are at least possible. In 2022, a lady arrived and the building's receptionist called Cracknell to meet her.

"She said she was running for president of Somalia," he said. "Initially I didn't believe her." However, the lady explained her background – growing up in Somalia in a politically active family – and showed Cracknell existing media stories about her campaign. She was passionate and articulate, and the paper ran her story with the headline: "Enfield woman on mission to bring peace to Somalia." Her campaign was ultimately unsuccessful, but what about the campaign to revive local newspapers? After the landslide of cuts and closures, a coalition of internet-savvy local journalists and resourceful community projects offers a more hopeful future – with the odd-walk-in thrown in for old times' sake.

CONCLUSION
Past, present and future

LOCAL NEWS HAS TAKEN A KICKING. During scores of interviews for this book, no one disputed that office closures and staff cuts have changed almost everything. Like many journalists, I saw this transformation in real time – and it spurred me to search for alternative employment. When I joined the *Dorking and Leatherhead Advertiser* as news editor in 2010, we had a Dorking office, three reporters and two part-time editorial staff working on regular features such as our Yesteryear local history pages. We also had access to a shared pool of photographers. By the time I left just three years later, things were very different. During that period, the management presented each negative step as an unavoidable hardship we must all endure. Looking back, I think the process was far more deliberate than that. And the same thing was happening almost everywhere.

Newspaper offices closed far and wide from about 2010 onwards. It's still happening, although the big firms are running out of offices to shut. In March 2021, Reach PLC said it would close all but fifteen of its offices. Archant did a round of closures that December, saying "very low numbers" of staff had returned to office-based working after Covid. I lost count of the cuts and closures announced while I wrote this book. So many experienced journalists were dumped out of work, and so many enthusiastic young reporters were sacked when they had barely started – or never found jobs in local news at all.

One announcement sticks in my memory. In November 2023, Reach announced 450 more job cuts. As the company's CEO gave a statement via livestream, staff were able to post anonymous comments. One wrote: "Your salary could pay for 174 journalists earning what I am. Are you taking a pay cut to save costs?" Another stated that the previous round of redundancies had left them suicidal. It's a tremendous credit to the passion and dedication of local journalists that there's anyone left at all.

It must be noted that local news organisations found themselves in a horrible situation after the 2008 financial crisis, when a sudden decline in advertising revenue collided with the unstoppable rise of online news and social media. Local papers, radio and TV were no longer the key sources of information for the areas they served.

All of the above has damaged local journalism almost everywhere. In some places it has disappeared entirely, leaving "news deserts". Research into this by City, University of London found local Facebook groups are now the default source of information in many British towns. Some users of these groups described the content as "toxic" and "racist", but said they provided the best source of up-to-date information.

These Facebook groups have many useful functions, but they are not a like-for-like replacement for the local paper. Journalists have to check their facts, and are trained in crucial areas including media law. They are also accountable to the communities they serve. On Facebook, anyone with a rumour or an unfounded accusation can post it. Laws on things like defamation and contempt of court still technically apply, but in practice legal action is rare.

Some local news websites try to keep up with the social media juggernaut by publishing absolutely everything instantly. Two-line nibs about a road closure appear alongside what would once have been called page leads. Some would argue these sites are poor, especially due to the snowstorm of pop-up adverts that can make it impossible to read the stories.

I agree, but local news is a tough product to sell in the age of YouTube and TikTok. Fierce online competition incentivises clickbait and churnalism (churning out pre-packaged stories from press releases), sometimes leaving little space for anything else. That's terrible for people, society and democracy, and it deprives young journalists of a vital (and highly enjoyable) training ground.

But – BUT! – good journalists and therefore good journalism still exist. Fewer reporters now prowl the streets or sit in the back of courts and council chambers, but some do. In conducting the interviews for this book, I've been heartened to find so many excellent and dedicated journalists still plying their trade in age-old ways: knocking on doors, making phone calls and generally dealing with all the glorious weirdness the public can offer. Training courses continue to send eager young reporters out into the world, to begin their career-long search for stories. They graduate into a very different journalistic environment than the one I joined in 2007, but people haven't changed that much – so stories are still there to find and to tell, if you know where to look.

And there are new places to look. Connections and contacts will always be the core of a journalist's job. That requires speaking to people – in person, ideally –

but the digital world provides unlimited information, unlimited stories. That can be great for local news, if used in moderation. Some local titles clearly source their stories almost entirely online, with their staff basically expected to sit at their desks and generate clicks. But many of those interviewed for this book stressed the importance of doing the basics properly: call your contacts, check your facts, remember what matters to your readers.

At first glance, today's "digital native" reporters have little in common with those behind community titles like *Greater Govanill* and the *Enfield Dispatch*. However, as I jumped back and forth through these interviews over many months, I saw more and more similarities between them. Their methods are different, but their goal is the same: to provide proper local news. I hope new business models will allow more journalists to defect to the new breed of community papers – leaving giant firms and their click targets behind.

That challenge is immense, but determined and resourceful people are working on it. The collapse of long-standing local papers was driven by money: they depended on selling newspapers and advertising space, and both streams dried up. But people still want and need local news. The void left by local newspapers created an accidental experiment, and the results could be surprising.

Those results might even include a journalist based in an office near you, ready for whatever the public can throw at them (metaphorically, I hope). That's where this book began – in the not-so-distant past, when anyone, almost anywhere, could interrupt a journalist. Those journalists didn't always enjoy the experience, but hundreds replied when I tweeted about the subject.

In the many interviews, letters, emails and tweets that made this book a reality, the enthusiasm of journalists – both past and present – was the common thread. Many said they felt lucky to do that job, whether for a year or half a century. Describing their triumphs and disasters – sometimes from several decades ago – people spoke a little faster, keen to describe these treasured scenes. I could almost smell the "smoke-befuddled" office of the *Acton Gazette* in 1979, hear the printing presses rolling at the *Bucks Herald* in 1991, and see Robert Barman trying to peel a man's glued hands from the *Kent Messenger*'s counter in 2003.

Which takes me back to my own memory of Antonio Massimo, the "aubergenius" whose visit cemented my fascination with walk-ins and began the long journey that led to this book. In more ways than he or I could have known at the time, he saw the future. By watching his allotment, he had noticed our changing climate – a major focus both for journalists and the wider world today. I have thought about Mr Massimo many times over the years. His remarkable energy influenced my own environmentalism and love of nature. I now work as a press officer for the University of Exeter, promoting climate and environmental research. I've even grown a few aubergines.

By walking into the *Crawley News* with his vegetables, Mr Massimo demonstrated his eccentricity and gave us a classic local newspaper story – the kind of quirky tale that makes people laugh at local papers. But, like so many of the walk-ins in this book, his story contained something more significant – something about community, about people and the stories they need to tell. I can vividly remember standing on his allotment, staying out of shot as our photographer took pictures. Mr Massimo beamed at the camera, proud of his bountiful garden. Googling his name as I wrote this conclusion, I discovered he died in 2022 at the age of 91 – a great age, no doubt made possible by a lifetime of activity, positivity and healthy eating. Part of me regrets the fact I never saw him after I left the *Crawley News* in 2010. But that's journalism. You cover stories and – for better or worse – you move on.

In the case of Mr Massimo, I will always be glad that he – like so many others at so many papers over so many years – walked through our door with a story to tell.

APPENDIX: TWEETS

I DIDN'T HAVE TIME or space in this book to interview everyone who replied to my original tweet about walk-ins. What follows is a selection of the best replies – those that work as one-liners. They're organised (as far as possible) to reflect the relevant chapters of the book. All are published with the permission of the people who posted them. Enjoy!

Chapter one: Legless killer, lock-switch dad & kidnapped tortoise

@acailler: "The strange lady who shouts at the photocopier is back again. She's asked for you."

@garytaphouse: We had a reader who was absolutely furious about the opening of a new lap dancing club, appalled at the shocking state of a society in which such brazen sexualisation of women was normalised. Turned out his misplaced rage was over a nib I'd written about a new line dancing club.

@SteveH_Citizen: My favourite was the guy who came into @leamobs office and said he'd been appointed by the Bishop of Birmingham to solve all of the social problems in the Midlands. Said bishop had actually not replied to his email and he had taken this as his approval. Write that one.

@Catcopywriting: When I was at the Evening Press (York) we had a tannoy system, if the reception staff saw us struggling with someone who had walked in they would do a building-wide announcement saying we were urgently needed back in the newsroom. A true service to local journalism…

@JBlount80: We had a code word, from memory. Reception would use it when they called downstairs to the newsroom to say someone was at front desk to talk about a story, when it was clearly nonsense.

@rwhitehouse13: Most memorable for me was the chap who came in saying he had created a design for a proposed new shopping centre in the town with the idea of a rotating restaurant at the top. He said he had carved a model of it out of cheese.

@ShokerMotion: We had a security guard who would take messages at reception and then run through the newsroom waving the piece of paper shouting "frrront paaage!" in a strong Brummie accent. They were usually just a nib at best.

@gfosterjourno: I had 2 blokes break into a fight each claiming the other was the Yorkshire ripper.

@chrislepkowski: "There's a bloke in reception who smells. Can you come and talk to him please?"

@haztastical: Came in to complain about various problems, including the fact they'd moved Kidderminster closer to Redditch than it used to be.

@haztastical: Oh and the man who came in to show me how long he could stare at the sun for.

@BelfastGonzo: I'll never forget the anti phone mast campaigner who left me her mobile number if I needed to get in touch.

@daveblackhurst3: I was once first back from lunch at the Stoke Sentinel to be told by n/desk to see 4 ppl in reception. To my horror they weren't together and had come in with 4 different stories. I had to set up a queuing system and didn't get back to newsroom til about 4pm.

@Kcl_Dan: I once had a guy walk into the office @elystandard complaining the shops in town didn't stock trousers for tall men. Deadly serious.

@DebbieWtravels: I had a woman ranting about 'foreigners' parking (quite legally) in her road. Turned out she meant people from outside the town, which takes racism to a whole new level. She didn't know I'd parked there that morning myself.

@NevWilson: An Elvis fan walked in to complain about dirty bollards on the A25 despite his repeated calls to the council… he posed up with a broom like The King for our snapper. He later posted a bar of soap to their HQ by way of protest. The package was destroyed over fears it was a bomb.

@TomOBMorris: Gloucestershire Echo 2004: "Batman's in reception for you again." The joys of covering Fathers 4 Justice.

@Jgibbins: "Can someone pop down? There's a woman in reception who has found a Lithuanian living in her shed." She had, and it went national…

Chapter two: Show and tell: Stoneless roses, Edna's medal & grenade at Greggs

@JoyPersaud: The receptionist, a friend, took details and summoned me. A bloke, who looked credible, had found a prehistoric skull – it was covered in… dirt and was the right shape, etc. He wanted to tell the Brit Museum. Turned out it was a rock… (I did write it up).

@StreetboyTim: Was… handed a VHS by an irate customer which he had bought via the small ads, which turned out to be a porno he was complaining was "terrible quality".

@JoeRobinson11: As a trainee [at] The Gazette in Blackpool a guy once asked me if I wanted to meet his father and then put a pot of ashes on the table. He also claimed to be blind and wanted stories done about discrimination against him because of it. He drove to the office.

@scribblydave: "There's a woman at the front desk says she's found a Cadbury's Nibble shaped like a, well…, best come and see for yourself…"

@pwnolan: I won't ever forget the day a man came into reception claiming he had found the world record biggest beef schnitzel. He had ordered it at the local pub, thought it was huge and so brought it into the office asking us to take a pic and write the yarn. A week or two later the same guy returned to the office saying that there was a kangaroo in our car park. I gently ushered him outside thinking he was off his tree again and making shit up. Then, bugger me dead, I saw a kangaroo in the car park!

@diannebourne: "Dianne, there's a man in reception with the world's smallest mouth organ… he wants to play it for you."

@MsAshleyDavies: An old gent insisted on giving me a presentation of his genius water-saving invention. It was a block of wood to put under one side of the washing-up bowl so you could wash up in the corner. I was the obits editor.

Chapter three: Animal, vegetable or mineral? Deadly jam, lucky duck & Nazi greyhound

@laurenpotts: "Lauren, there's someone in reception who wants to see you. She says her dog's 'found a big stick. Really big. Taller than me'." Pontefract, Sept 2012.

@DaveFeatures: Man walks in with a ferocious-looking spider in a tub. Super, I thought – tale of terror and good pic. "No, I'm not interested in a story. I want you to identify it. I've already been to [the] council and they were worse than useless." Man shrugging. Man walks out, with the spider.

@EEkirstie: Working in a rural newspaper office alone, I had some hilarious, weird, sometimes creepy, walk-ins. Highlights included the time a guy came in to gift me a bucket of frogspawn and said "just call me Barry the frog".

(image credit: Kat Harbourne)

@KatHarbourne: Mine is a radio station but still applies: "There's a woman in reception with a stuffed badger".

@coyknorth: Bloke walked up stairs into our district office and plonked boxes of tortoises on my desk. Told me he'd read my piece on urgent need to reinvigorate coastal economy of Whitley Bay. A tortoise zoo would have them flocking in – badly needed a pic story that day, so ran with it.

@LiamRandallLDR: I was once asked to have a chat with an old lady who brought a tiny white dog into the old Leader office in Wrexham, claiming it could sing. Walked into the meeting room highly sceptical, but my god did it do a passable attempt. Its voice was quite haunting and high pitched.

@thisislaurent: A call-in not walk-in – to a woman saying there was a Big Cat ("ooh I think it could have escaped from a zoo") in her tree. I was SENT OUT despite my protestations. Turned out to be… a big cat.

@igaeilge: A woman came into our office – we had no reception as such – and told me she had been away for the weekend. When she returned her goldfish was frozen. She chopped the ice containing the goldfish out of the bowl, put it on the frying pan and melted the ice. The fish survived.

@RobertFisk: If I didn't let the facts get in the way of the story I'd say a man turned up unannounced with a massive mushroom. But, truth be told, he'd phoned beforehand and I convinced him to bring it in.

@NickEvansAuthor: I am reminded of the time a chap walked into reception at Sheerness about 12 years ago with a pair of reptiles on leads. They were smaller than crocodiles but bigger than newts! It had taken him nearly an hour to walk them from the car parked 150 metres away.

@ImSuzanneLeigh: I had: "There's someone in reception with a massive slug." They weren't wrong.

@Reedyberg: When I worked at the Dorset Echo someone found a corn snake and brought it into reception for us to sort out.

@britpopcyclist: At the Islington Gazette, reception rang up to say a woman was in to collect the stuffed lion she had won. Nobody could remember a stuffed lion competition. Cue a mass lion search for a good 20 minutes before it emerged that she had won tickets to the Stuff Live Exhibition.

Chapter four: Too good to be true? Bin Laden in Skegness

@DavidSpereall: The man who came in and said he hadn't breathed for 20 years, which he claimed had been confirmed by his doctor. He said… that to demonstrate it, he needed two people to come round his house.

@rozlaws: I remember someone telling us at the Rugby Advertiser that Salman Rushdie was hiding out in the town at the height of his fatwah. Could have been true, he went to Rugby School. Sadly never found him.

@Catcopywriting: One walk-in woman seemed ok at first until she told me the Queen and John Major were trying to kill her to keep her quiet. When I finally (politely) got rid of her, she screamed 'you've just missed out on the best story of your career'. I mean, who knows, maybe she was right!

@KevinPashby: Mine is radio related. A man once turned up to tell us he'd died and had come to talk to us from "the other side". I asked him if he'd seen my Nan and he walked out.

@bobdale7: The story goes that John Logie Baird took his invention of TV to a national paper and a junior reporter was sent to fob him off, having been told "there's someone in reception who thinks he can make radio with pictures. Get rid of him."

@PollitaMarch: There was that woman from the X Factor who used to come in weekly to say Simon Cowell loved her despite being ridiculed for her bad singing. Julie at front desk used to warn me so I could crawl out the back door.

@Lord_Alfreston: Guy insisted he could make clouds disappear by just looking at them. He was deadly serious, made me go outside with him so he could show me. Triumphant when a wispy cloud disappeared despite me trying to explain evaporation. He was worried he might do it to a plane as well!

Chapter five: The walking dead: Mortality mix-ups

@rob15959: I saw a compositor use his scalpel to remove a death notice after the undertakers phoned the office to say "sorry, been a mistake; that one's still flapping".

@JtQuinn1: There was the… woman who turned up at York Street (our reception) and told me she'd just come back from the dead. That's all. Sadly for her, the front page had already gone to print otherwise I'd have definitely shouted for someone to hold it.

Chapter six: Reporters under fire: Hostage, handcuffs & 'fuck you too!'

@LLBruce: A furious man came, annoyed at my use of a generic, headless pic of a belly hanging out, outside a Gregg's. He was adamant it was his hairy bulge and I did not ask his permission. Had to track down source who assured him the midriff in question was from Croydon not Boro.

@kimberleybarber: The man who walked into the office really cross: "I'm told I'm in your paper". And he was – the front page court snatch after being fined for being really cross (criminal damage). I had to slide the copies under the counter and plead ignorance.

From Tristan Harris (via @robgeorge1): "I want to complain… I'm in your paper as a convicted arsonist."
"Well sir you did appear in court didn't you? Charged with arson…"
"Yes."
"And how did it end sir???"
"I was guilty."

@jabberingjourno: My vaguely critical takeaway review – furious manager turns up in reception and thrust cold curry in my face to prove that they can make it better – his normal chef had been off sick. I actually ate a bit.

@steveclarketv: Southern Evening Echo '71. Hell's Angels Eastleigh Chapter are in reception. "Where's Steve Clarke? He's quoted us saying the Southampton chapter have 'the intelligence of a clothes peg on a line'. They want to kill us." I had. Our beefiest reporter was sent to note their concerns.

@vywi: Call in from a woman who said local kids were bullying her because of her wig. I went to her house, and asked how it all started. "Well… it was right after I stabbed my social worker." I made my excuses, etc…

@tomedwardsbbchw: The time a chap insisting he was Fred West's cousin came to see me at the Gloucester Citizen, circa 2010. Steaming drunk, he tried to give me a story about his relation being "misunderstood", before proceeding to eat a copy of the newspaper's front page and walk about.

@neilchandler: Local drug dealer, known as the Codfather (this was Grimsby) upset with our court coverage. Reason he had petrol in bedroom, he explained, was not to dissolve gear if raided, as CPS claimed, but to pour over any rivals he'd threaten with a match if they dared to have a go.

@patrickcullen01: Got nabbed to cover reception… one lunch time and a lady came in and threw her phone bill at me followed by copies of the paper – she ran up a massive phone bill on the dating page and blamed me!

@DavidJWhetstone: Outraged rockers in to complain about the pop column (Doncaster Evening Post, late 70s). Aged sub had changed every "he" to "she" in a story about Alice Cooper.

@AlanGreenwood_: V angry man who insisted on speaking to The Editor. We'd run a story about his brother's court case. Brother had thrown a pot of boiling water at 15 y-o stepdaughter. Nasty. Man was furious because the report stated his brother was a joiner when he was actually a carpenter. Sample line: "MY PARENTS ARE SO EMBARRASSED BY YOUR MISTAKE THAT THEY WON'T LEAVE THE HOUSE." He left, vowing to take the matter up with the PCC (Press Complaints Commission). Never heard about it again, thank goodness.

Chapter seven: The ones that count

@davidmbarnett: The saddest one was an old woman and her dog who turned up telling me she'd been sleeping rough for a week in winter. I didn't write a story but took her to the council's housing office and got her sorted.

@TYDCreative: Nursing home worker wanted coverage for open day. During chat she mentions they've applied for a resident's WW2 medals. He'd never been able to receive them because he was homeless for many years. Incredible life story, brill feature. Medals arrived in time for Remembrance Day.

@JadeWright: Eternal gratitude to the reception staff at the papers I worked on. On my first newspaper job one woman quietly rang 999 while I kept a man talking as he threatened to take an overdose standing there in reception. He came back and thanked us as it got him the help he needed.

Lynne Walsh via email: We ran a story of an elderly woman, either mugged or defrauded. There wasn't a "someone" in reception, but an envelope left, marked with the victim's name. It had a considerable sum of money – and a note that said simply: "Dick Turpin."

Chapter eight: Ring-ins & letters: Siege negotiator, stolen scarecrow & battle-tank surprise

@barbaraargument: Caller; Settle a bet for the lads down the pub will you. Who's that journalist with the long red nails who appears on Question Time? Me; Err, Ann Leslie? Caller; That's her. Click.

@JayneHowarth: One of many: a phone call when I was on the 6pm-1am shift at The Birmingham Post on a Friday. Man calls to tell me his takeaway chicken has feathers in it. He wanted the police involved.

@Jackie_Novels: Not a walk in, but an elderly woman read my byline in the paper and wanted to comment on the story. She went through the phone book, called my parents with the same surname, and spent half an hour sharing her viewpoint with my confused mother. They went ex-directory after that.

@stevehollis75: Not a walk-in but had a phone-in once at the Islington Gazette where a lady claimed the reason she crashed her car was due to an exploding can of condensed milk. Went off like a bomb apparently!

@Nige1Chapman: News editor: "There's someone on the line who says he's got a teepee in his garden. What's your extension Richard?" Richard: "233." Fellow reporter Steve's phone rings.

Chapter nine: On patch: Brothel knocking, Croydon Christmas & pirates hate Britney

@simonaldra: Reporter I know had a long gaming session in the evening. When he took off his headset, there was a lot of commotion outside. He opened the curtains, finding several police cars, ambulances and a fire truck outside. Guy had stabbed someone, then set fire to his apartment.

Chapter ten: Twin terrors: Death knocks & vox pops

@chrislepkowski: How many did similar with a death knock? "I tried the door 10 times, looked through the windows, but nobody answered…" Reality: went around the block, saw it looked rough, popped into a pub for a swift half. Will make up some cock & bull story for the news editor.

@jimdruryE20 (on death knocks): The worst part of a cub reporter's job, for sure. I remember once when an elderly couple had been killed in Spain in the crossfire of a gun battle. I asked their next door neighbour for a tribute. She said "the lord works in mysterious ways" and shut the door!

@SteveH_GSA (recalling being on work experience): I had to ask people in Birmingham city centre what they thought about the clocks changing that weekend. One guy just looked at me and said "are you taking a the piss out of me!" – I still think the guys at Birmingham Mail were having me on.

@JohnHyde1982: First ever job was to vox pop the people of Jaywick after a national newspaper called their town a dump. Knocking on doors, asking if they agreed. I was 16, had to get the bus there. Should point out the people I spoke to were brilliant, so helpful and kind and willing to speak.

@oflo12: I once tried to vox pop John Terry, who'd just come out of the stationery shop carrying a big piece of card. He wasn't interested in talking about the general election.

@TheWislon: (Filming for local TV in Southampton) Me: Hello, we're from Southern TV, may I ask if…

Man (roughly shoving cameraman aside): The lady with me is not my wife, fuck off mate.

AUTHOR'S NOTE

THANK YOU FOR READING. Like many books, this began as a labour of love, then became a hateful burden, before becoming fun again. Finally, it got finished. I sincerely thank every current or former journalist who contributed, whether via a single tweet or in multiple interviews. Special thanks to Sam Blackledge and Michael Connellan: former colleagues, interviewees and sanity checkers when I could no longer make sense of the words.

Thanks above all to Hannah, without whom nothing would happen. And to the kids, without whom this would have been finished years earlier (but with far fewer fun diversions).

If you enjoyed this book, please tell people about it – as publicly and frequently as possible. If it has inspired you to share a story or an opinion about local news, find me on social media or email alex.morrison@hotmail.co.uk.

If you've grown a massive vegetable, I probably can't help you – but maybe your local paper would like to see it.

Printed in Great Britain
by Amazon